Tax Policy Reforms
2021

SPECIAL EDITION ON TAX POLICY DURING THE COVID-19 PANDEMIC

OECD
BETTER POLICIES FOR BETTER LIVES

This work is published under the responsibility of the Secretary-General of the OECD. The opinions expressed and arguments employed herein do not necessarily reflect the official views of OECD member countries.

This document, as well as any data and map included herein, are without prejudice to the status of or sovereignty over any territory, to the delimitation of international frontiers and boundaries and to the name of any territory, city or area.

The statistical data for Israel are supplied by and under the responsibility of the relevant Israeli authorities. The use of such data by the OECD is without prejudice to the status of the Golan Heights, East Jerusalem and Israeli settlements in the West Bank under the terms of international law.

Please cite this publication as:
OECD (2021), *Tax Policy Reforms 2021: Special Edition on Tax Policy during the COVID-19 Pandemic*, OECD Publishing, Paris, *https://doi.org/10.1787/427d2616-en*.

ISBN 978-92-64-62565-5 (print)
ISBN 978-92-64-72850-9 (pdf)

Tax Policy Reforms
ISSN 2617-3425 (print)
ISSN 2617-3433 (online)

Foreword

This report provides an overview of the tax measures introduced during the COVID-19 crisis since the outbreak of the pandemic. It is an update to the report that was presented at the G20 Finance Ministers' Meeting held on 15 April 2020. The aim of the report is to provide an overview of how tax measures have evolved since last year and identify the key tax policy trends across countries.

The report is primarily based on countries' responses to a questionnaire that was circulated in January 2021 by the OECD to all members of the OECD/G20 Inclusive Framework on Base Erosion and Profit Shifting.[1] The questionnaire requested information on countries' tax responses to the COVID-19 crisis across corporate income taxes (CIT) and other business taxes, personal income taxes (PIT) and social security contributions (SSC), value added taxes (VAT) and excise duties, environmentally related taxes and property taxes. Data was collected from 66 countries, including all OECD and G20 countries, and 21 additional Inclusive Framework members that replied to the OECD questionnaire.[2]

The report also offers some policy guidance as to how tax policy responses could be adapted to address short term challenges. It identifies guiding principles on how countries can improve the targeting of emergency relief and carefully withdraw it as they emerge from the grip of the pandemic and loosen mobility and other restrictions. It also provides some guidance on how to design and implement effective stimulus-oriented tax measures.

The report contains three chapters: Chapter 1 provides an overview of the macroeconomic background and forecast across OECD and G20 countries. Chapter 2 gives an update on the tax measures introduced by countries in response to the COVID-19 crisis. Chapter 3 provides some forward-looking guidance on ways to address tax policy challenges in the short run and a brief overview of the work that the OECD will be undertaking in the future to help countries reassess their tax and spending policies in the longer run.

This report was produced by the Tax Policy and Statistics Division of the OECD's Centre for Tax Policy and Administration. It was led by Sarah Perret and written jointly by Patrice Ollivaud (Economics Department), Gioia De Melo, Daniel Fichmann, Sarah Perret and Richard Clarke (Centre for Tax Policy and Administration), with inputs and supervision from Bert Brys. The authors would like to thank the delegates of Working Party No.2 on Tax Policy Analysis and Tax Statistics for their inputs. The authors would also like to thank David Bradbury for his guidance and acknowledge the helpful contributions and comments received from Piet Battiau, Sveinbjorn Blondal, Luisa Dressler, Peter Green, Tibor Hanappi, Sebastian Königs, Nigel Pain, Jonas Teusch, and Sébastien Turban. The authors are also grateful to Erwan Cherfaoui, Hiroko Matsui and Michael Sharratt for their help with the database of tax measures and to Karena Garnier, Hazel Healy and Carrie Tyler for their assistance with formatting and communication.

Table of contents

FIGURES

TABLES

Follow OECD Publications on:

http://twitter.com/OECD_Pubs

http://www.facebook.com/OECDPublications

http://www.linkedin.com/groups/OECD-Publications-4645871

http://www.youtube.com/oecdilibrary

http://www.oecd.org/oecddirect/

This book has...   *StatLinks*
A service that delivers Excel® files from the printed page!

Look for the *StatLinks* at the bottom of the tables or graphs in this book. To download the matching Excel® spreadsheet, just type the link into your Internet browser, starting with the *https://doi.org* prefix, or click on the link from the e-book edition.

Executive summary

Scope of the report

The report has been prepared for G20 Finance Ministers and Central Bank Governors (FMCBG). The report updates the OECD report on *Tax and Fiscal Policy in Response to the Coronavirus Crisis,* which was presented to the G20 FMCBG in April 2020.

This report provides an overview of the tax measures introduced during the COVID-19 crisis across almost 70 jurisdictions since the outbreak of the pandemic. The report covers all OECD and G20 countries, and 21 additional jurisdictions that replied to a questionnaire that was circulated in January 2021 by the OECD to all members of the OECD/G20 Inclusive Framework on Base Erosion and Profit Shifting. It examines how tax policy responses have varied across countries and evolved over the last year.

The report also offers some guidance as to how tax policy responses could be adapted to address the short-term challenges countries face. In particular, it identifies some guiding principles on how countries could improve the targeting of emergency relief and implement recovery-oriented tax measures as they emerge from the grip of the pandemic and loosen mobility and other restrictions. It also gives a brief overview of the work that the OECD will be undertaking in the future to help countries reassess their tax and spending policies in the post-crisis environment.

Key economic and tax policy trends

The outbreak of COVID-19 has resulted in a global health crisis and sharp decline in economic activity that are without precedent in recent history. In just a few months, the COVID-19 pandemic turned from a health crisis into a global economic crisis whose full extent is still unfolding one year later. The COVID-19 pandemic caused a much larger contraction in global GDP than the global financial crisis in 2008, reaching nearly 10% in the first half of 2020 and an estimated 3.4% overall in 2020. A recovery has begun, but is far from complete.

The successful development and gradual deployment of effective vaccines has significantly improved prospects for a durable recovery, but uncertainty remains high. The latest OECD *Economic Outlook* projects global GDP growth of 5.6% in 2021 and 4% in 2022. Nevertheless, substantial uncertainty remains. A significant rebound in economic activity depends on the effective roll-out of vaccines across the globe and the continuation of supportive fiscal and monetary policies to boost demand. With the virus and its variants continuing to spread, targeted restrictions on mobility and activity may need to be extended or reintroduced as new outbreaks occur, which could limit the pace of recovery.

There are also increasing signs of divergence across countries, sectors and households. Extended containment measures and mobility restrictions will hold back growth in some countries and service sectors in the near term. Additional factors could lead to diverging outcomes across countries and regions, including differences in the pace of vaccinations and in the degree of policy support. Households have also been unevenly impacted by the crisis, with those on low-incomes, women and younger generations suffering higher economic costs. Without enhanced policy measures, both fiscal and structural, there are strong risks that the recovery could be unequal in both pace and scale across households, firms and countries.

Government responses to the crisis have been unprecedented since the onset of the pandemic. The scale of government support to households and businesses has varied, but it has reached unparalleled levels in many countries. Fiscal packages have often consisted of a wide variety of measures including loan guarantees, job retention schemes, direct transfers, expanded access to benefits and tax measures. Strong and timely fiscal support has played a vital role in supporting incomes, preserving jobs and keeping businesses afloat.

As part of these broad fiscal packages, tax measures have played a significant role in providing crisis relief to businesses and households. In the first half of 2020, in response to broad-based lockdowns in many countries, the focus of tax measures was almost exclusively on providing emergency relief. Last year's report on *Tax and Fiscal Policy in Response to the Coronavirus Crisis* highlighted that many tax measures were aimed at alleviating businesses' cash flow difficulties to help avoid escalating problems such as the laying-off of workers, the temporary inability to pay suppliers or creditors and, in the worst cases, business closure or bankruptcy. Countries also introduced tax measures to support households, although other tools including direct transfers and expanded access to social benefits often played an even more prominent role in providing direct relief to households.

Many of the tax measures introduced in the initial stages of the crisis have been prolonged, with some being modified to channel support to the households and businesses most affected by the crisis as it has evolved. Some countries have expanded eligibility for relief to beneficiaries initially not covered by the measures or increased the generosity of initial relief measures. As the pandemic has progressed, some countries have increased targeting to ensure that support is better directed towards those that are most severely affected, especially where governments have moved away from broad-based lockdowns towards more selective and targeted containment measures.

Tax packages have also evolved, with an increasing focus on recovery-oriented stimulus measures[3] to supplement the crisis relief provisions introduced in the early stages of the response to the pandemic. As lockdowns and other containment measures began to ease after the first wave of the pandemic, countries started introducing recovery-oriented tax measures, including in particular corporate tax incentives for investment as well as reduced VAT rates targeted at hard-hit sectors. In most countries, these stimulus measures have co-existed with prolonged relief measures.

Another significant trend observed over the last year is that an increasing number of countries have introduced or announced new tax increases. Unlike in the emergency phase of the crisis, a number of countries reported tax increases in the second half of 2020 and early 2021. While a few of these tax increases involved one-off or temporary measures, most are intended to be permanent. Among these longer term tax increases, some represent a continuation of pre-crisis trends, such as increases in fuel excise duties and carbon taxes, which were the most common tax increases reported by countries. On the other hand, some tax increases mark a departure from pre-crisis trends. In particular, a number of countries introduced tax increases on high-income earners, including increases in top personal income tax (PIT) rates reported in seven countries and the move from flat to progressive PIT systems in the Czech Republic and Russia. In addition, in contrast with the trend towards lower statutory corporate income tax (CIT) rates in recent decades, the United Kingdom has announced a CIT rate increase from 19% to 25% for profits above GBP 250 000 from April 2023.

Despite some common trends, there have been notable differences across regions and countries regarding the scope and types of tax packages, in part reflecting the varying prevalence of the virus and different containment approaches. Countries with severe lockdown policies have generally introduced more comprehensive tax support measures, while countries adopting less restrictive containment measures have generally introduced fewer COVID-19 related tax relief measures. The types of tax measures introduced by countries have also partly reflected the timing of virus outbreaks. For instance, in the Asia-Pacific region, many of the countries that were at the epicentre of the pandemic in late February and early March 2020 have managed to effectively contain the virus, and have subsequently introduced more stimulus-oriented tax measures than other countries that are still grappling with large numbers of infections.

The scope and scale of tax policy packages has also reflected countries' fiscal space and their ability to rely on central bank support. Some developing and emerging countries entered the crisis with more limited fiscal space, especially in Africa and Latin America. In addition, some developing and emerging countries have not been able to use monetary policy in response to the crisis in the same way as advanced economies have. Overall, many developing and emerging economies have had less room to provide fiscal support to households and businesses than other countries. The report generally finds that countries with higher tax-to-GDP ratios have introduced larger and more comprehensive tax packages.

Tax policy responses have reflected other country-specific factors. The types of measures introduced have depended on the architecture of countries' tax systems. For example, there has been less income support to households via the PIT in emerging and developing countries as most low-income earners are not subject to PIT in these economies. More generally, where tax bases are narrow, countries have had less room to provide support or stimulus via the tax system. The size of the informal sector and governments' administrative capacities have also influenced the scope and form of tax support. Finally, with only a few exceptions, so far announced tax increases have been concentrated in OECD countries, possibly reflecting the fact that they are among the countries that have introduced the most generous support packages.

Way forward

A key priority in the short run will be to improve the targeting of tax relief to ensure that support is channelled to those who need it most and to carefully withdraw it where it is no longer needed. The report highlights the importance of avoiding the premature withdrawal of relief but of increasingly targeting it to severely affected businesses and households. Maintaining support for highly impacted households is essential to mitigate the unequal impact of the crisis and reduce risks of increased poverty. Similarly, relief should remain available for businesses in severely constrained sectors. Targeting has become more feasible with increasing information on the economic and distributional impacts of the crisis. For those sectors where support is being withdrawn, this should be done carefully to avoid sudden spikes in tax burdens or "cliff-edge" effects, for instance by progressively phasing out support. Where support is extended, this should be done in ways that avoid storing up problems for the future, for instance by favouring "soft-landing" approaches, such as converting tax deferrals into interest-free tax instalments.

As economies reopen, fiscal stimulus, including through well-designed tax measures, could play a significant role if economic activity remains sluggish. Recovery-oriented stimulus policies should be considered if consumption and investment remain persistently low when containment measures are lifted and activities are allowed to resume. Larger and more prolonged stimulus measures might be needed where recovery is anaemic. However, where economies rebound strongly, the size and length of stimulus packages may need to be curtailed as stimulus measures could have pro-cyclical effects if they are maintained once economic recovery is on a solid footing. More generally, there will be a need for continued policy flexibility, as continued restrictions are making conventional stimulus policies somewhat less effective and the timing of policy implementation more difficult.

In order to be effective, stimulus policies need to be carefully timed. Introducing recovery-oriented stimulus measures while strict restrictions are still in place could be ineffective and could even undermine the primary health objective of containing the spread of the virus. In fact, there is evidence that some of the tax stimulus measures introduced after the first wave of the pandemic have had less of an impact than anticipated because they were introduced when restrictions were still in place or because they encouraged greater social interactions.

Stimulus measures should be temporary and targeted at the areas where equity needs and fiscal multipliers are likely to be highest. Temporary stimulus encourages businesses and households to bring their spending and investments forward and limits the impact on public budgets. Ensuring that stimulus measures are temporary may require having clear end-dates (with possibilities for temporary extensions) or tying their duration to the achievement of certain outcomes (e.g. economic recovery in specific sectors, level of employment). In addition, stimulus policies should be targeted at areas where they are most likely to generate additional consumption and investment. For instance, untargeted tax measures to support household consumption would partly subsidise spending that is likely to occur anyway, especially among higher income households who have accumulated additional savings during the pandemic and will be eager to consume once restrictions are lifted. On the other hand, income support targeted at less affluent households would have higher multiplier effects, in addition to being more progressive. Regarding corporate taxation, expenditure-based tax incentives tend to generate greater additional investment than profit-based ones.

Governments should also prioritise measures that support labour market recovery and business recapitalisation. Given the unprecedented job losses resulting from the crisis and the risks of long-term scarring effects on labour markets, tax measures could be used to encourage businesses to retain their workers and hire new employees. For instance, temporary and targeted reductions in employer social security contributions could be considered. To mitigate the impact of the crisis on companies' capital structure and solvency, tax measures could also be used to support business recapitalisation. Measures could include temporary schemes allowing companies to exempt part of their profits by recording them under a capital reserve aimed at rebuilding their equity. Such schemes could be capped and targeted at SMEs, and accompanied by strict rules to prevent any abuse. It is important to note, however, that while tax measures can be helpful instruments, non-tax measures will likely play a more critical role in supporting employment and business recapitalisation.

Tax stimulus measures should be aligned with longer-term environmental, health and social objectives. Stimulus policies could simultaneously support recovery and the attainment of longer-term objectives. For instance, targeted support for promising clean technologies could encourage recovery and help accelerate the transition to a carbon-neutral economy, especially if it is combined with greater carbon pricing efforts. Special tax incentives could also be granted to support businesses adapting their workplaces or facilities to strengthened sanitary protocols. Finally, stimulus should be aligned with social objectives and avoid regressive impacts.

These guiding principles can be useful across countries, but well-designed stimulus packages will naturally need to be tailored to countries' specific circumstances. Stimulus packages will need to be calibrated to the size of countries' output declines and the removal of their containment measures. Stimulus should also be aligned with countries' means and take into account their fiscal space. While limited stimulus may result in a slower recovery, disproportionate stimulus packages compared to countries' available fiscal space may undermine market confidence, which could weigh on the recovery. However, the near-term fiscal space of many countries has risen thanks to declining debt servicing costs and growth is often a major contributor to fiscal sustainability.

While the short-term priority is to effectively navigate the pandemic and build a robust and inclusive recovery, countries will need to start thinking about whether their public finance strategies are capable of meeting the medium and long-term challenges they face. Once the recovery is firmly in place, the post-crisis environment will provide an opportunity for countries to undertake a more fundamental reassessment of their tax and spending policies along with their overall fiscal framework. Such a reassessment will need to take into account both the challenges brought to the fore by the crisis as well as those related to ongoing structural trends, including climate change, rising inequalities, digitalisation and population ageing. The OECD will be undertaking significant work in the future to help countries reassess their public finance policies to support inclusive and sustainable economic growth in the longer term.

Notes

[1] In some cases, the responses provided by countries to the questionnaire has been complemented with additional information from other sources.

[2] The additional 21 Inclusive Framework members that responded to the OECD questionnaire are: Albania, Andorra, Barbados, Bulgaria, Croatia, Honduras, Jersey, Macau, Mauritius, Nigeria, Republic of North Macedonia, Panama, Paraguay, Peru, Seychelles, Singapore, Thailand, Trinidad and Tobago, Tunisia, Turks and Caicos, and Uruguay.

[3] Broadly speaking, stimulus can refer to all discretionary fiscal policy actions beyond automatic stabilisers, including for instance higher government spending on health, income support schemes and tax relief measures. In this paper, however, references to stimulus measures should be understood as recovery-oriented measures, whereas measures aimed at providing income and liquidity support are referred to as relief measures.

1 Macroeconomic background

This Chapter provides a general assessment of the macroeconomic situation and outlook. It covers trends in growth, industrial activity, trade, investment, the labour market, public finances and inflation, based on the *OECD Economic Outlook, Interim Report March 2021*. This background is useful to understand the context in which the tax measures discussed in the report were adopted (Chapter 2), but also to identify how tax policy responses may need to evolve in the future (Chapter 3).

1.1. The COVID-19 crisis has been large and widespread

The COVID-19 pandemic continues to have widespread effects on economies and societies. The onset of the crisis saw sharp declines in output in all economies, with the virus spreading around the world. Global output declined by almost 10% in the first half of 2020, a much more rapid and deeper hit than in the global financial crisis (Figure 1.1). The subsequent rebound in output has been stronger than expected, but is far from complete. Output in all countries remained well below the levels expected prior to the pandemic at the end of 2020 (Figure 1.2), with shortfalls of 4¾ and 4¼ per cent in OECD and global GDP, respectively. Without the prompt and effective policy support introduced in all economies to cushion the impact of the shock on household incomes and companies, output and employment would have been substantially weaker.

Figure 1.1. The COVID-19 crisis was deeper than the global financial crisis

Real GDP growth, year-on-year

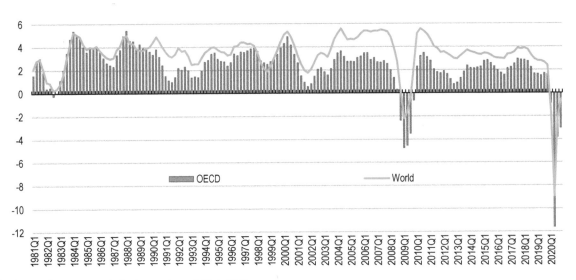

Note: Aggregates are computed using moving weights in PPP.
Source: OECD Economic Outlook database.

StatLink ᵃˢ℄ https://stat.link/8wft41

Figure 1.2. The estimated output loss from the COVID-19 crisis is large and widespread

Difference between GDP in 2020Q4 and pre-pandemic projections, per cent

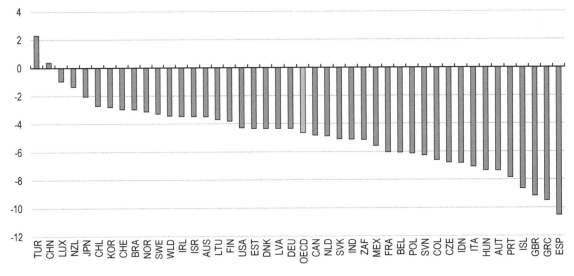

Note: The value corresponds to the difference for the last quarter of 2020 between the latest data and the projection for GDP in the last quarter of 2020 made in the November 2019 OECD Economic Outlook.
Source: OECD Economic Outlook database.

StatLink ᵃˢ℄ https://stat.link/3psw4k

Almost all major countries experienced a year-on-year decline in GDP in 2020. Ireland, China and Turkey were exceptions, helped by lower restrictions on activity and strong fiscal or quasi-fiscal measures, and, for Ireland, strong IT and pharmaceutical exports from the multinational sector. The pandemic affected

China initially, but its economy recovered quickly too, helped by stronger infrastructure spending and strong export growth. Many other Asia-Pacific economies also coped relatively well with the crisis due to spillovers from China and to more effective testing, tracking and tracing policies to reduce virus transmissions. Argentina, Mexico, South Africa, India and most European countries were relatively more affected than elsewhere. This reflects extended disruptions from renewed virus outbreaks and associated reductions in working hours in many service sectors. The different sector specialisation of economies also affected growth, with the economies most dependent on international travel and tourism generally experiencing a larger GDP decline in 2020. All in all, in 2020, global and OECD GDP are estimated to have declined by 3.4% and 4.8% respectively.

Despite further COVID-19 outbreaks in the latter part of 2020, activity was stronger than expected. Containment measures and the associated declines in mobility had a smaller adverse impact on activity than in the early stages of the pandemic. In part, this may reflect a more careful targeting of public health measures and income support. Recent restrictions have focused largely on service sectors with high levels of direct contact between consumers and producers, with manufacturing and construction activities generally affected only mildly. Global industrial production has thus continued to strengthen in recent months and global trade has now returned to pre-pandemic levels (Figure 1.3), supported by the strong demand in IT equipment and medical supplies. However, the impact of a new series of restrictions towards the end of 2020 and the beginning of 2021, affected service sector activities and household consumption in many countries, and slowed the momentum observed in the third quarter of 2020.

Figure 1.3. Industrial activity and trade are rebounding but service sectors have lost momentum

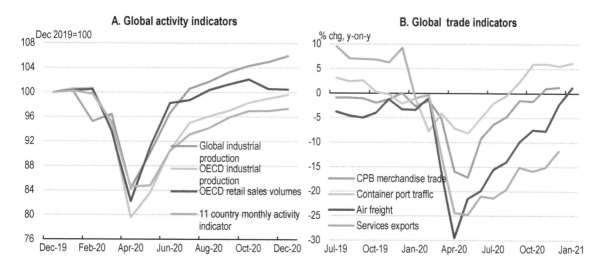

Note: Data in Panel A are PPP-weighted aggregates. The retail sales measure uses monthly household consumption for the United States and the monthly synthetic consumption indicator for Japan. The 11-country activity indicator uses GDP or economy-wide output data for Argentina, Brazil, Canada, Chile, Colombia, Finland, Japan, Korea, Mexico, Norway and the United Kingdom. Data in Panel B are all in volume terms apart from services exports, which are an aggregate of monthly nominal USD exports in 38 countries.
Source: OECD Economic Outlook database; CPB; IATA; RWI/ISL Container Throughput Index; WTO; and OECD calculations.

StatLink https://stat.link/lk9bxw

1.2. The recovery has been rapid in some sectors but lagged behind in others

Business survey indicators suggest that manufacturing activity has been particularly buoyant in recent months, including in the euro area and the United States. For services sectors, the situation is more varied with growth observed for some economies while restrictions continue to weigh on activity in other economies, notably in Europe. In particular, activity remains well below pre-crisis levels for hospitality and leisure services despite a significant improvement in other sectors since the trough in April 2020 (Figure 1.4).

Figure 1.4. Output remains depressed for sectors directly facing restrictions

Percentage difference from February 2020

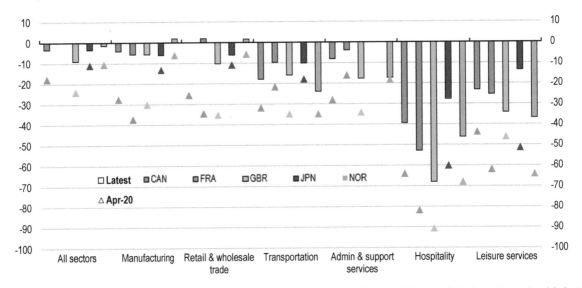

Note: Monthly GDP in Canada, Norway and the United Kingdom, monthly output in Japan and France. Data based on national industrial classifications. Data on all sector output are not available for France, and data on administrative and support services are not available for Japan. Transportation data for Norway exclude ocean transport. Latest data are for January 2021 in Norway and the United Kingdom, and December 2020 in the other countries.

Source: Office of National Statistics, United Kingdom; Ministry of Economy, Trade and Industry, Japan; Insee, France; Statistics Canada; Statistics Norway; and OECD calculations.

StatLink 🔗 https://stat.link/jw8ehl

The crisis had a significant impact on gross fixed capital formation, with a large fall in the first half of 2020 across most countries (Figure 1.5). Despite continued uncertainty, investment has rebounded in several economies, for example in Australia, Canada and the United States, with volumes close to pre-crisis levels at the end of 2020. Equipment investment has been strong in several countries, helped by new investments in the IT equipment and systems needed for remote working. Housing investment has also picked up, helped by favourable financing conditions. Substantial government support has also helped many firms to stay in business and helped to ensure the continued availability of external finance. Nonetheless, this carries risks, as some supported firms may ultimately prove unviable, and higher leverage on corporate balance sheets could be a medium-term drag on firms' ability to operate and invest.

Figure 1.5. The recovery in gross fixed capital formation has been mixed

Index 2015 Q1 =100

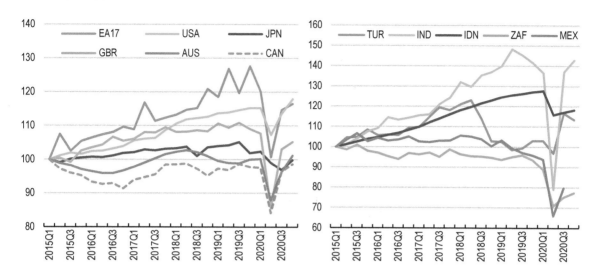

Note: EA17: Euro area (17 OECD countries).
Source: OECD Economic Outlook database.

StatLink https://stat.link/zh7se0

1.3. The labour market has shown some resilience but could be affected in the longer term

In the aftermath of the crisis labour markets remain weak, but the impact on unemployment has been relatively contained so far (Figure 1.6). Although activity at the end of 2020 was well below the pre-pandemic level in many countries, the OECD-wide unemployment rate was only 2 percentage points higher than at the end of 2019. Massive government support programmes helped to maintain jobs in many OECD countries, preventing workers from losing their jobs while their workplaces were shut. The United States did not implement particular employment-supporting programmes, and the US unemployment rate surged by nearly 10 percentage points in the second quarter of 2020 before falling quickly as the economy re-opened. In several OECD countries, notably in Europe, the claimant unemployment rate through 2020 barely changed and even decreased slightly in France and Italy. Nonetheless, the employment rate declined in almost all OECD countries over the year to the fourth quarter of 2020, dropping by 1¼-percentage points in the median economy.

The labour market crisis particularly affected women, who tend to work more in services such as hospitality and tourism that have been subject to strong containment measures. During 2020, the female unemployment rate increased more sharply than the male unemployment rate in many OECD countries (Figure 1.7). However, the situation changed during 2020: for example, in the United States, where unemployment surged in the second quarter, the female unemployment rate increased by an additional two percentage points compared to men, before it declined faster for women in the rest of the year.

Figure 1.6. The increase in unemployment has been contained

Change in the unemployment rate between 2020Q4 and 2019Q4, in percentage points of the labour force

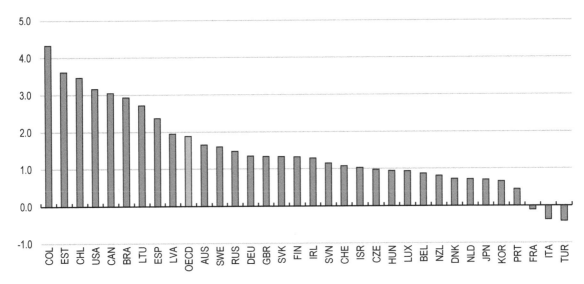

Source: OECD Economic Outlook database.

StatLink https://stat.link/h73eoa

Figure 1.7. The increase in female unemployment has been relatively sharp

Difference in the year-on-year increase of the unemployment rate in 2020Q4 between women and men, in percentage points of the labour force

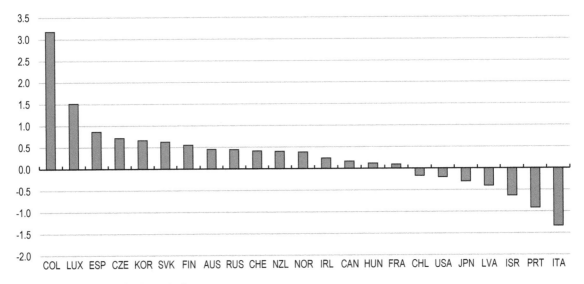

Source: OECD, Labour Market Statistics database.

StatLink https://stat.link/tczh9u

The employment situation remains particularly vulnerable in sectors with close contacts between consumers and producers, with total hours worked remaining significantly below pre-pandemic levels (Figure 1.8, Panel A). The crisis is likely to require some labour and capital reallocation from unviable businesses to growing ones, although the extent remains uncertain. Some sectors most affected by physical distancing requirements and associated changes in consumer preferences may be permanently smaller after the crisis. A lasting shift towards remote working, reductions in business travel and the increasing digital delivery of services, including e-commerce, could also change the mix of jobs available and the location of many workplaces (Figure 1.8, Panel B).

Figure 1.8. Part of changes in the labour market could become permanent

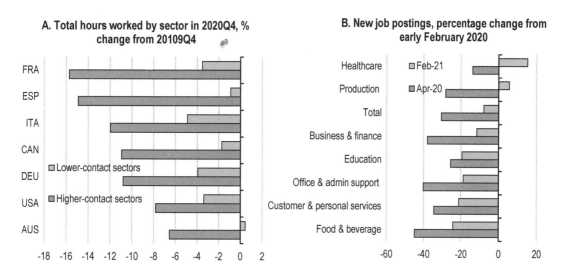

**A. Total hours worked by sector in 2020Q4, %
change from 20109Q4**

**B. New job postings, percentage change from
early February 2020**

Note: In Panel A, high-contact sectors are ones with high social interactions between consumers and producers. These include retail and wholesale trade, accommodation and food services, transportation and storage, arts and entertainment, and other personal services. Data in panel B are seasonally-adjusted online job postings by type of occupation and aggregated over 20 countries. April 2020 and February 2021 respectively refer to the weeks 24-30 April 2020 and 21-27 February 2021.
Source: OECD Economic Outlook database; Bureau of Economic Analysis; Statistics Canada; Australian Bureau of Statistics; Statistics Bureau, Japan; Eurostat; Office for National Statistics; Indeed; and OECD calculations.

StatLink 🔗 https://stat.link/o130c9

With the fall in activity and higher unemployment, real labour compensation declined by around 2% for the OECD as a whole in 2020 (with a fall of 0.7% in nominal compensation) (Figure 1.9). The fall was particularly large in the euro area (above 3%), and smaller in the United States (about 1%). This reflects lower employment in 2020 and a composition effect that varies according to the size and the degree of protection of jobs in low-wage sectors. For example, in the United States, the increase in unemployment was higher, and more low-wage workers lost their jobs, giving a positive compositional effect on economy-wide compensation per employee.

Figure 1.9. Labour compensation fell across the OECD

Real labour compensation growth rate, in per cent

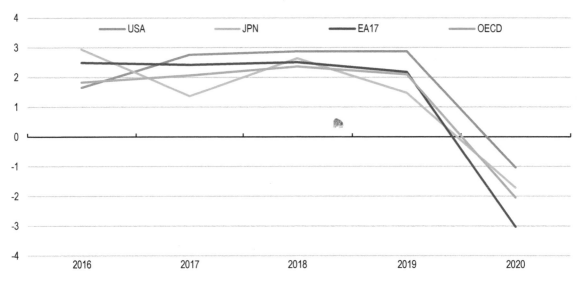

Note: EA17: Euro area (17 OECD countries). Total labour compensation (wages plus social security contributions) deflated by the private consumption deflator.
Source: OECD Economic Outlook database.

StatLink 🖴🖪🖪 https://stat.link/nuhkl4

1.4. Fiscal policy has played a major role during the crisis

Strong and timely fiscal support since the onset of the pandemic has played a vital role in supporting incomes and preserving jobs and businesses. Estimates for the OECD as a whole in 2020 suggest an increase of 5 percentage points of GDP in the primary deficit adjusted for the economic cycle (a measure of the fiscal stance); and an increase of nearly 17 percentage points of GDP for gross public debt (Figure 1.10). These increases were particularly significant in the United States but smaller in the euro area.

Figure 1.10. Public finances deteriorated quickly in 2020

Estimates based on projections

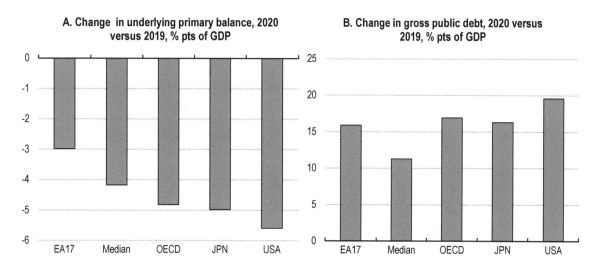

A. Change in underlying primary balance, 2020 versus 2019, % pts of GDP

B. Change in gross public debt, 2020 versus 2019, % pts of GDP

Note: EA17: Euro area (17 OECD countries). Projections based on information available as of November 2020. Median refers to the median OECD country for the associated metric. Public debt refers to the Maastricht definition for the euro area.
Source: OECD Economic Outlook 108 database.

StatLink ᐧ https://stat.link/gq4nhk

Notwithstanding the substantial rise in government liabilities, debt-servicing costs remain low, helped by the space provided by very accommodative monetary policy. For example, in Canada, gross public debt increased by nearly 35 percentage points of GDP in 2020 while gross interest payments remained the same. Government bond yields declined in 2020 as the monetary policy stance became more accommodative (Figure 1.12), but have begun to edge up as prospects for a stronger global economic recovery have improved. Amongst major emerging-market economies, the fall in interest rates was also generalised during 2020. There has been a recent increase for China, which recovered earlier from the crisis.

The extent of fiscal support is likely to vary significantly across economies over the next two years, with substantial extra spending in the United States (Box 1.1), and to a lesser extent Japan and Canada, but limited discretionary measures in others. This is particularly so in Europe, unless already agreed spending plans at the level of the European Union are implemented earlier than anticipated. Nonetheless, budget deficits will remain large, as appropriate, and the automatic fiscal stabilisers should be allowed to operate fully. The initial broad support to the whole economy will need to evolve towards more targeted support to the hardest-hit sectors as the recovery progresses, facilitating labour and capital reallocation from sectors facing structural demand weakness.

Box 1.1. The American Rescue Plan

In December 2020, a package of measures worth USD 900 billion (4% of GDP) was introduced, which boosted household incomes and, to a smaller extent, consumer spending at the start of 2021. The American Rescue Plan of USD 1.9 trillion (about 9% of GDP), which passed Congress in March 2021, provides a considerably larger additional stimulus that should raise aggregate demand substantially in the United States, with welcome spillovers for activity around the world. The main provisions of the Plan are:

- Direct USD 1400 payments to households. The payments will phase out above earnings of USD 75,000 for individuals and USD 150,000 for a couple. Initial total costing: USD 425 billion.
- Financial aid to state and local governments. Initial total costing: USD 370 billion.
- Supplementary unemployment benefits of USD 300 per week will be extended until 6 September. Initial total costing: USD 290 billion.
- Childcare and schools support. Initial costing: USD 357 billion.

Illustrative simulations on the NiGEM global macroeconomic model suggest that the measures in the American Rescue Plan could raise US output by around 3-4 per cent on average in the first full year of the package (from 2021Q2 to 2022Q1) (OECD, 2021[1]). The US upturn also helps to stimulate demand in all other economies, and would boost global GDP by around 1% during this period.

The near-term impact of the US fiscal package is relatively large with backward-looking consumers, reflecting the greater sensitivity of their spending to current income developments and the impact of higher government transfer payments. In contrast, forward-looking consumers, more focused on the lifetime income path of incomes and the potential budgetary offset from higher tax payments in the future, spend less of the stimulus. Nonetheless, in both scenarios, there are substantial near-term gains to US output, and the risk of lasting supply-side damage from a slow recovery from the COVID-19 pandemic has been reduced considerably.

Figure 1.11. The GDP impact of the American Rescue Plan will be sizeable

Percentage difference on average from baseline over first four quarters

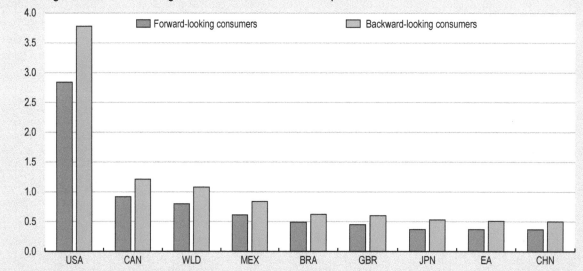

Note: The chart shows the average percentage difference in GDP relative to baseline over the first full year of the package (2021Q2-2022Q1). Simulation of the planned fiscal stimulus in the United States set out in the American Rescue Plan. The new measures are worth up to USD 1.9 trillion (around 8 ½ per cent of baseline GDP). Measures are assumed to take effect over 2021Q2-2022Q2. Policy interest rates remain unchanged in the United States and other advanced economies until mid-2022, but are endogenous in the emerging-market economies.

Source: OECD calculations using the NiGEM macroeconomic model.

StatLink https://stat.link/8wofua

Figure 1.12. Accommodative monetary policies pushed down 10-year government bond yields during 2020

Percentage points change

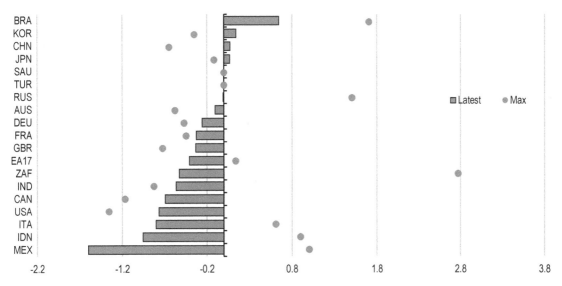

Note: "Latest" refers to the change between end-2019 and the latest available data up to 20 February. "Max" refers to the maximum change since end-2019. Based on a 10-day average of daily observations.
Source: Refinitiv; and OECD calculations.

StatLink ᵐᵗˢᴾ᭴ https://stat.link/0yhgto

1.5. The outlook highlights the risk of divergence across economies

The successful development and gradual deployment of effective vaccines has improved prospects for a durable recovery significantly, provided steps are taken to ensure that such vaccines are deployed fully throughout the world, and supportive fiscal and monetary policies continue to underpin demand. Nevertheless, uncertainty is still high, with the virus and its variants continuing to spread across the globe, and the possibility of further targeted restrictions on mobility and activity being implemented as new outbreaks occur. Such restrictions would check the pace at which the most affected service sectors and tourism-dependent economies can rebound.

The March 2021 OECD Interim Economic Outlook projects global GDP growth of 5.6% for 2021 and 4% for 2022. However, the recent signs of increasing divergence across economies may persist. Many factors could lead to diverging outcomes across regions: differing pace of vaccination deployment; varying degrees of policy support; uneven scope to lower accumulated saving; and the sector specialisation of economies.

Overall, the global economy is expected to recover to its pre-pandemic output level by mid-2021 (Figure 1.13). This milestone was attained in the fourth quarter of 2020 for the G20 emerging-market economies as a whole, thanks to the strong recovery in China and Turkey. In contrast, GDP in some economies, may only surpass the fourth quarter of 2019 level at the end of 2021 or well into 2022. The economic impact of the pandemic and its aftermath remains well contained in many Asia Pacific economies, reflecting effective public health measures, and the significant regional boost provided by the upturn in industrial activity and the rebound in China. Additional fiscal support will also help the recovery in Japan and India. In the United States, strong fiscal support should strengthen demand substantially and enable a stronger recovery from the pandemic, with beneficial spillovers for other economies, particularly

Canada and Mexico. A more gradual upturn appears likely in the major European economies, reflecting continued containment measures in the early part of 2021 and more limited fiscal support, although the acceleration of vaccine deployment should help momentum to build, particularly in the United Kingdom. Emerging-market economies in Latin America and Africa are also facing a renewed resurgence of the virus, and the slow pace of vaccine deployment and limited scope for additional policy support is likely to moderate the recovery.

The longer the period before the adult population is vaccinated in all countries, the longer the global crisis will last, accentuating economic costs and the risk of lasting scarring effects. Vaccination rates vary greatly across countries, slowing the pace at which their economies can fully reopen (Figure 1.14). A faster pace of vaccination will allow restrictions to be lifted earlier for some countries, such as Israel, the United Kingdom and the United States, while easing is expected to come later in 2021 for others, notably in continental Europe. The global deployment of vaccinations is crucial if all restrictions to mobility and social interactions are to be lifted entirely.

Figure 1.13. Economies are projected to rebound at different rates

Real GDP relative to 2019Q4

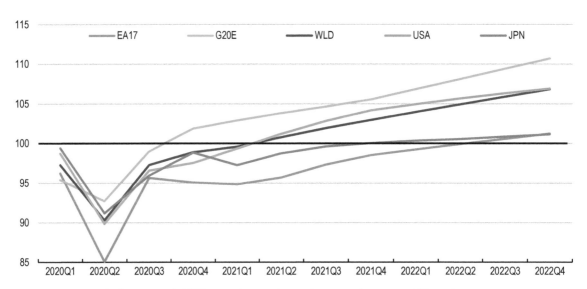

Note: EA17: Euro area (17 OECD countries). G20E stands for emerging-market economies that are G20 members.
Source: OECD Economic Outlook database.

StatLink https://stat.link/j5yhlo

Detailed scenarios highlight the large risks around the growth outlook. If vaccine production and deployment are not fast enough to stop virus transmissions, global GDP growth could be reduced by close to 1 percentage point in 2021 and 1¼ percentage point in 2022. Confidence would remain weak for longer and spending would slow, especially if renewed restrictions during the latter half of 2021 were to be required. This downside scenario would raise the chances of long-lasting costs from the pandemic. Alternatively, on the upside, a faster pace of vaccination production and deployment would hasten relaxation of containment measures, boost consumer and business confidence, and lift global GDP growth by 1½ and 1 percentage point in 2021 and 2022 respectively, taking it to 7% and 5%.

Figure 1.14. The pace of COVID-19 vaccination deployment differs substantially across countries

Per hundred people, 17 March 2021 or latest available

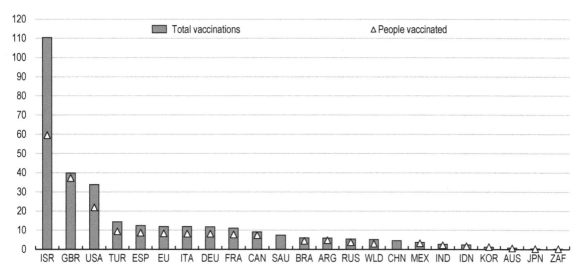

Note: 13 March for Australia; 15 March for France; and 16 March for Germany and the United Kingdom.
Source: Our World in Data vaccination database, accessed March 18, 2021.

StatLink 🔗 https://stat.link/p0lwej

1.6. Prospects for a full recovery depend on restoring consumer confidence

One condition for the recovery to fully materialise is the use of cumulated household saving for consumption. Household saving rates in 2020 rose well above pre-crisis levels (Figure 1.15, Panel A). The rise was due both to precautionary – standard in a period of crisis – and involuntary factors, with spending, notably for certain services, constrained for several months. There are also delays before stronger government income support to households feeds into higher consumption.

At the beginning of 2021, consumers remained cautious, in part due to continued confinement measures in many countries, and confidence was still below pre-pandemic levels (Figure 1.15, Panel B). The deployment of vaccines should gradually restore confidence as the pandemic eases, helping to reduce precautionary saving and free pent-up demand, but the pace at which this will occur is uncertain. This highlights the need for a fast and worldwide vaccination rollout.

Figure 1.15. Higher household saving can translate into higher future demand if confidence rises

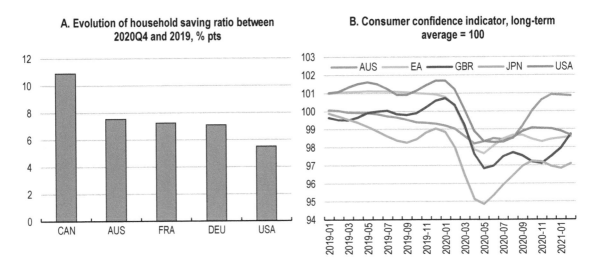

A. Evolution of household saving ratio between 2020Q4 and 2019, % pts

B. Consumer confidence indicator, long-term average = 100

Source: OECD Economic Outlook database; Insee; and OECD Main Economic Indicators database.

StatLink 🔗 https://stat.link/ayj5wq

1.7. Headline inflation receded during the crisis but cost pressures have recently increased

The annual headline inflation rate eased during 2020 and by the end of the year was zero or negative in China, Japan and the euro area, and 1% in the United States (Figure 1.16). Although supply disruptions associated with the pandemic were apparent in the prices of some goods and services, the forces weighing on aggregate demand around the world dampened underlying price pressures through most of 2020. Global commodity prices were also at low levels throughout much of 2020 as well.

Some of these factors have started to unwind as the recovery has progressed, and headline inflation has begun to pick up. By February 2021, the headline inflation rate reached 1¾ per cent in the United States and 1% in the euro area (year-on-year). Commodity prices as well as survey-based measures of input prices have recently risen (Figure 1.17). Oil prices are now broadly in line with their 2019 average, and food and metals prices have reached levels last seen in the early 2010s. Supply shortfalls have emerged in some sectors, as the global recovery was faster than anticipated while it takes time to restore full capacity. Shipping prices in certain regions have increased sharply especially from China.

Some sectors, notably semi-conductors, have also experienced difficulties in meeting the demand from the rapid and global recovery in manufacturing. Nonetheless, underlying price pressures still generally remain mild in the advanced economies, reflecting sizeable spare capacity and still weak labour markets, and temporary price pressures in particular sectors should gradually abate. Amongst the emerging-market economies, inflation is expected to increase more in net commodity importers. Price pressures could also increase if domestic currencies were to depreciate due to higher capital inflows attracted by rising relative returns in the United States.

Figure 1.16. Headline inflation decreased through 2020

Year-on-year percentage change

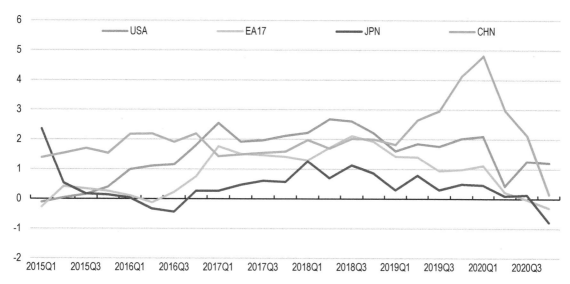

Note: EA17: Euro area (17 OECD countries).
Source: OECD Economic Outlook database.

Figure 1.17. Cost pressures have recently begun to increase

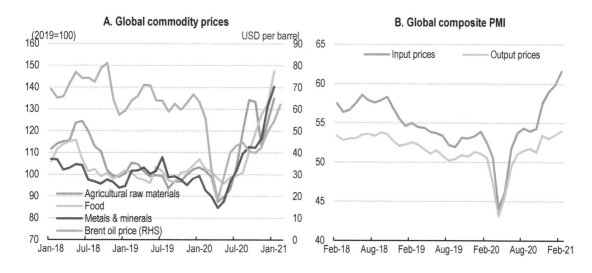

Source: Refinitiv; and Markit.

References

OECD (2021), *OECD Economic Outlook, Interim Report March 2021*, OECD Publishing, Paris, [1]
https://dx.doi.org/10.1787/34bfd999-en.

2 Update on the tax measures introduced during the COVID-19 crisis

This Chapter provides an update on the tax measures adopted by countries during the COVID-19 crisis. It starts by providing an overview of the tax measures introduced in 2020 and early 2021 in the 66 countries and jurisdictions that replied to the 2021 OECD Tax Policy Reform Questionnaire, highlighting their evolution over time as well as differences across countries. It then provides a more detailed description of changes to corporate income taxes and other business taxes (section 2.2), personal income taxes and social security contributions (section 2.3), VAT/GST and excise duties (section 2.4), environmentally related taxes (section 2.5) and property taxes (section 2.6).

2.1. Overview of tax measures during the COVID-19 pandemic

Countries' fiscal packages in response to the COVID-19 crisis have been unprecedented in both size and scope in many countries. As discussed in Chapter 1, strong and timely fiscal support since the onset of the pandemic has played a vital role in supporting incomes and preserving jobs and businesses. In January 2021, the IMF estimated that global fiscal support had reached close to USD 14 trillion (IMF, 2021[1]).

Fiscal packages have contained a wide variety of measures. Key measures to provide liquidity support to businesses have included loan guarantee schemes, where the government guarantees all or part of the value of bank loans granted to eligible businesses. Many OECD countries also introduced new or expanded job retention or wage subsidy schemes to prevent mass unemployment (see Box 2.1), but these schemes were notably less common outside of the OECD. Income support for households was primarily provided through direct transfers to households, rather than through tax systems, given the need to deliver support as quickly as possible, and through expanded access to social benefits, including for non-standard workers who typically benefit from more limited social protection than regular employees (see Box 2.1).

Box 2.1. OECD and G20 governments took unprecedented action to support jobs and workers during the COVID-19 crisis

OECD and G20 countries responded rapidly to the crisis with unprecedented levels of emergency support to keep households and companies afloat, protect jobs and incomes, and prevent their economies from collapsing. Some of the main work and income-support related measures included:

- *Providing paid leave to sick and quarantined workers*: Paid sick leave has played a central role in the fight against the pandemic. It has helped mitigate the spread of the virus by permitting sick workers and those with COVID-19 symptoms to self-isolate, while protecting their incomes, jobs and health. Many OECD and G20 countries substantially expanded paid sick leave policies during the initial phase of the crisis. In Korea, for example, which does not have a mandatory paid sick-leave scheme in place, the 2015 Epidemic Act extended paid leave to workers who are hospitalised or quarantined because of COVID-19. The United States introduced two weeks of mandatory sick pay for workers with COVID-19 related symptoms for companies with less than 500 employees, which expired at the end of 2020. Several countries increased paid sick leave entitlements for workers with COVID-19 symptoms or those quarantined, often through the introduction of new pandemic-related payments or top-ups, including Australia, France, Italy and Spain.

- *Supporting jobs and companies through job retention schemes*: Job retention schemes (JRS) have been one of the main tools for many OECD governments to prevent large-scale layoffs by companies heavily hit by the crisis. Through these schemes, governments pay (part of) the wages for workers whose hours are reduced because their employers experience a temporary reduction in business activity. This preserves workers' jobs and incomes, and it allows employers to hold on to their workers' talent and experience and to quickly ramp up operations again once economic activity recovers. A number of G20 economies, including Brazil, France, Germany, Italy, Spain and Turkey, already had JRS in place when the crisis struck. Many of these pre-existing schemes were expanded through simpler access, greater coverage, and more generous support paid to workers and employers. Some other G20 economies, including Australia and Canada, introduced new JRS. Across the OECD, take-up of JRS peaked at around 20% of dependent employment in April/May 2020, supporting approximately 60 million jobs, more than ten times as many as during the global financial crisis (see Figure 2.1).

- *Extending support for workers who lost their job or self-employment income*: In spite of governments' rapid measures to protect jobs and support companies, millions of workers across G20 economies have lost their jobs and incomes during the crisis. While unemployment benefit (UB) systems and other forms of income support helped prevent economic hardship for many workers affected by job loss, the crisis laid bare – or accentuated – a number of gaps in those schemes, particularly for workers on non-standard contracts. Many G20 countries therefore extended their UB systems during the current crisis, by improving access and coverage (e.g. France, Spain and the United States), extending benefit durations (Argentina, Germany, Italy and the United States), and raising benefit levels (Australia, Russia, the United Kingdom and the United States).

- **The crisis also created an immediate urgency to shore up support for workers and households not covered by earnings-replacement benefits** such as UBs or JRS, including many self-employed and informal workers. Several countries (such as Australia, Germany and Italy) facilitated access to existing minimum-income schemes to quickly channel additional support to low-income households. Spain introduced a new means-tested minimum living income (PIT exempt). Many countries introduced or expanded cash transfer schemes targeted at specific groups, notably the self-employed (e.g. Brazil, Canada, Colombia, France, Germany, Italy, Korea and the United Kingdom), and informal workers or undocumented migrants (e.g. Colombia, South Africa and the US State of California). A few countries (including Japan, Korea and the United States) made cash payments to (nearly) the entire population to help households make ends meet.

Figure 2.1. The use of job retention schemes was very high in some countries

Percentage of dependent employment (April/May 2020, September 2020, December 2020)

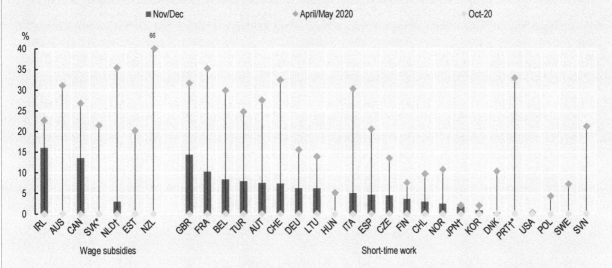

Note: Take-up rates are calculated as a percentage of dependent employees in 2020 Q1. Peak date refer to April/May for most countries (July for Canada, October for Japan). Wage subsidies are job retention schemes that provide financial support for hours worked, while short-time work refers to financial support for hours not worked by workers that remain employed by their employer. Japan, Netherlands, Portugal: Stocks are estimated as 3 months cumulative flows. Italy: Latest data are provisional estimates. United States: Refer to Work sharing benefits. Source: OECD (*forthcoming*), *Job retention schemes during the COVID-19 crisis*, Employment Outlook 2021

StatLink https://stat.link/o4m0d6

One year into the crisis and with vaccination programmes underway in many countries, it appears as though some of the worst economic consequences have been avoided or mitigated thanks to unprecedented and rapid government action. As a result, the future is beginning to look a little brighter, with the most recent OECD *Economic Outlook* projecting that global GDP could rise by 5.6% in 2021 (see Chapter 1). However, it is essential that governments continue to support households and businesses affected by the economic effects of COVID-19 in the near future, particularly given that new virus variants and the logistics of vaccination campaigns will require continued restrictions to economic activity. Millions of workers are still on job retention schemes, millions of others are unemployed or underemployed, and the financial situation of many firms has substantially weakened.

Source: OECD (2020) *COVID-19: From a health to a jobs crisis*. OECD Employment Outlook 2020, OECD Publishing, Paris, https://doi.org/10.1787/cea3b4f4-en

As part of these wider fiscal packages, tax measures have played a significant role in providing crisis relief to businesses and households. Tax measures have been particularly critical in providing liquidity support to businesses. Last year's report highlighted that many tax measures were focused on alleviating cash flow difficulties (OECD, 2020[2]) to help avoid escalating problems such as the laying-off of workers, temporary inability to pay suppliers or creditors and, in the worst cases, closure or bankruptcy. Countries also introduced tax measures to support households, although as mentioned above, other tools including direct transfers and expanded access to social benefits often played a more important role in keeping households afloat.

Many of the tax measures introduced in the initial stages of the crisis were prolonged, but some have been modified to channel support to the households and businesses most affected by the crisis. Some countries have expanded eligibility for relief to beneficiaries initially not covered by the measures (e.g. Italy, Lithuania and the United Kingdom) or increased the generosity of initial relief measures (e.g. Germany and Italy). As the pandemic has progressed, some countries have increased targeting to ensure that support is better directed at those that are most severely affected (e.g. Denmark, Greece, Italy, Indonesia, Japan, Portugal, Spain, Turkey and the United Kingdom), especially where governments moved away from broad-based lockdowns. Greater targeting of tax measures has been far less pronounced, however, than changes to the targeting of public support programmes such as wage subsidies and job retention schemes (OECD, 2021[3]).

Tax packages have also evolved to become more mixed, with recovery-oriented stimulus measures added to crisis relief provisions. In response to broad-based lockdowns in many countries in the first half of 2020, the focus of tax measures was almost exclusively on providing emergency relief to businesses and households. However, as lockdowns and other containment measures began to ease after the first wave of the pandemic, countries started introducing recovery-oriented tax measures (Table 2.1 and Figure 2.2). Common measures have included corporate tax incentives for investment as well as reduced VAT rates targeted at hard-hit sectors. In most countries, these stimulus measures have co-existed with prolonged relief measures.

Table 2.1. Typology of tax measures introduced in response to the COVID-19 crisis

	Relief	Recovery-oriented stimulus	Tax increases
Objectives of policies	Cushion the economic and social impacts of virus containment policies	Stimulate aggregate demand and investment	Finance part of the government response to the crisis
Main types of tax measures	<ul><li>Tax deferrals</li><li>Tax filing extensions</li><li>Accelerated tax refunds</li><li>Loss-carry back provisions</li><li>Temporary tax waivers</li><li>Temporary tax rate reductions</li></ul>	<ul><li>Tax incentives for investment</li><li>Reduced corporate or other business taxes</li><li>Tax incentives for employment</li><li>Temporary VAT rate reductions</li><li>Lower property transaction taxes</li></ul>	<ul><li>Increases in top personal income tax rates</li><li>Health excise tax increases</li><li>Environmental tax increases</li><li>Property tax increases</li><li>Business tax increases</li></ul>

Source: 2021 OECD Tax Policy Reform Questionnaire.

Figure 2.2. Most common tax measures across groups of countries

Shares of countries reporting tax measures in each group

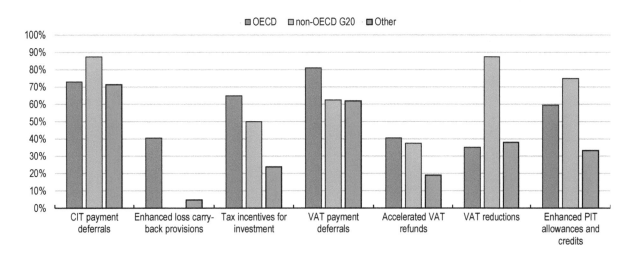

Note: The three groups of countries consist of 37 OECD countries, eight non-OECD G20 countries and 21 other countries and jurisdictions that are members of the OECD/G20 Inclusive Framework.
Source: 2021 OECD Tax Policy Reform Questionnaire

StatLink ᵐˢ▶ https://stat.link/81ek6b

Another significant evolution since last year's report is the number of countries that have introduced tax increases. Unlike in the emergency phase of the crisis, a number of countries reported tax increases in the second half of 2020 and early 2021. While a few of these tax increases were one-off or temporary, most were permanent. Among these longer term tax increases, some are a continuation of pre-crisis trends, such as increases in fuel excise duties and carbon taxes, which were the most common tax increases reported by countries (see Figure 2.6). On the other hand, some tax increases mark a departure from pre-crisis trends. In particular, a number of countries introduced tax increases on high-income earners, including increases in top PIT rates reported in seven countries and the move from flat to progressive personal income tax (PIT) systems in the Czech Republic and Russia. In addition, in contrast with the trend towards lower statutory corporate income tax (CIT) rates in recent decades, the United Kingdom has announced a CIT rate increase from 19% to 25% for profits above GBP 250 000 from April 2023.

Despite some common trends, there have been notable differences across regions and countries regarding the scope and types of tax packages, in part reflecting the prevalence of the virus and their containment approaches. Countries with severe lockdown policies have generally introduced more comprehensive tax support measures, while countries adopting less restrictive containment measures have introduced fewer COVID-19 related relief tax measures. The restrictiveness of lockdown policies has depended on various factors, including the prevalence of the virus, but also whether countries could afford to keep businesses and households afloat in lockdowns. The types of tax measures introduced by countries have also partly reflected the timing of virus outbreaks, with, for instance, countries in the Asia-Pacific region, which were at the epicentre of the pandemic in late February and early March 2020 and managed to effectively contain it earlier than other countries, introducing more stimulus-oriented tax measures, including investment tax incentives, than other countries (see Figure 2.3).

Figure 2.3. Most common tax measures in selected regions

Shares of countries reporting tax measures in each group

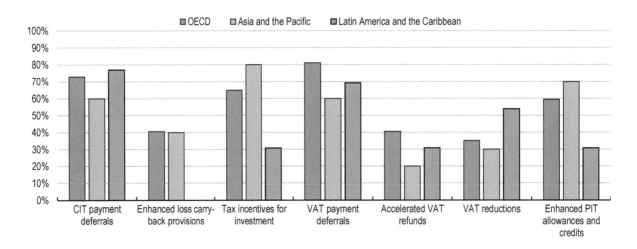

Note: OECD member countries in Asia and the Pacific and in Latin America and the Caribbean are included in both groups.
Source: 2021 OECD Tax Policy Reform Questionnaire

StatLink 🔗 https://stat.link/0yfb9w

The scope of tax packages has also reflected countries' fiscal space and their ability to rely on central bank support. Some developing and emerging countries collect low tax revenues as a share of GDP compared to other countries (see Figure 2.4) and had more limited fiscal space going into the crisis, especially in Africa and Latin America. In addition, developing and emerging countries have not been able to use monetary policy in response to the crisis as advanced economies have. Overall, many developing and emerging economies have had less room to provide fiscal support to households and businesses than other countries. As shown in Figure 2.2, tax packages in countries outside of the OECD and G20 have predominantly consisted of CIT and VAT deferrals, which have lower expected forgone tax revenue implications than rate reductions, exemptions and waivers. Figure 2.5 also shows that countries with higher tax-to-GDP ratios have introduced more comprehensive tax packages.

Figure 2.4. Tax-to-GDP ratios in the OECD, G20 and other surveyed countries and jurisdictions (2018)

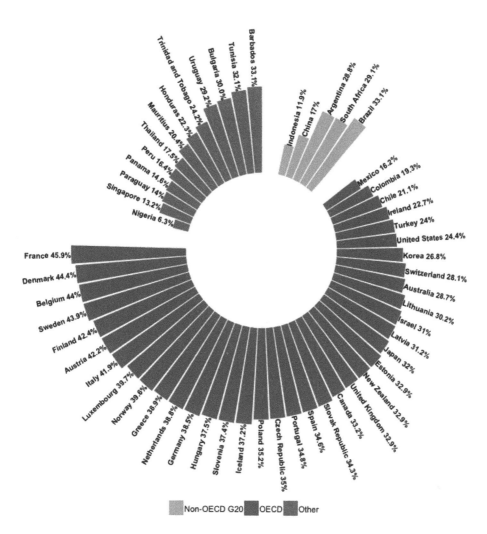

Note: Tax to GDP ratios from the OECD Revenue Statistics Database are missing for Albania, Andorra, Croatia, India, Jersey, Macau, Republic of North Macedonia, Russia, Saudi Arabia and Turks and Caicos. These countries and jurisdictions are therefore not included in this figure

Source: OECD Revenue Statistics Database

StatLink ᵐᵢₛ₁ https://stat.link/f4mnpe

Figure 2.5. Most common measures across countries with different tax-to-GDP ratios

Shares of countries reporting tax measures in each group

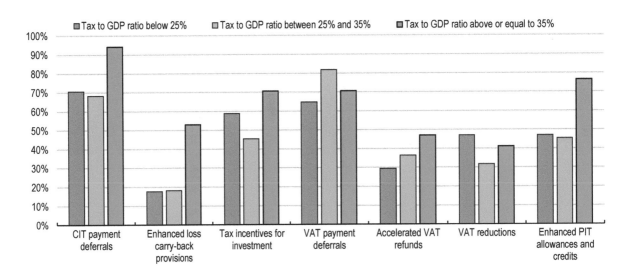

Note: Countries and jurisdictions are distributed into three groups (below 25%, between 25% and 35% and 35% and more) based on their tax to GDP ratios. Tax to GDP ratios are missing for Albania, Andorra, Croatia, India, Jersey, Macau, Republic of North Macedonia, Russia, Saudi Arabia and Turks and Caicos. These countries and jurisdictions are therefore not included in this Figure.
Source: Revenue Statistics and 2021 OECD Tax Policy Reform Questionnaire.

StatLink ᵃᵢₛᴸ https://stat.link/13gbaz

Tax packages have reflected other country-specific factors. The types of measures introduced have depended on the architecture of countries' tax systems. For example, there has been less income support to households via the PIT in emerging and developing countries as most poor people are not subject to PIT in these economies. More generally, where tax bases are narrow, countries have had less room to provide support or stimulus via the tax system. The size of the informal sector, by making it harder to reach the most vulnerable households and businesses, has also affected the amount and type of tax support provided by countries. The types of measures provided by countries were also influenced by governments' administrative capacities, as some support measures require more administrative capability and may be more vulnerable to abuse than others. The likelihood of introducing tax increases has also varied across countries. With a few exceptions, tax increases have been concentrated so far in OECD countries (see Figure 2.6), partly reflecting the fact that they generally introduced more generous support packages than other countries. Some tax increases, in particular environmentally and health related ones, were planned or announced before the COVID-19 crisis.

Figure 2.6. Reported tax rate increases and new taxes across all countries

Number of tax rate increases and new taxes introduced by group

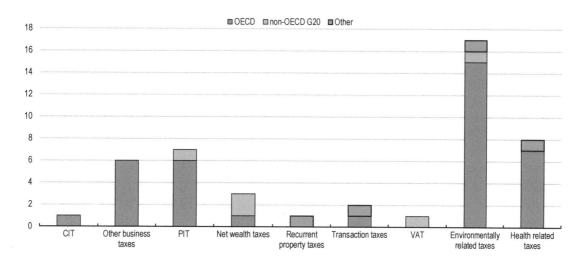

Note: The three groups of countries consist of 37 OECD countries, eight non-OECD G20 countries and 21 other countries and jurisdictions that are members of the OECD/G20 Inclusive Framework. Changes in import and export duties are not included in the graph.
Source: 2021 OECD Tax Policy Reform Questionnaire

StatLink https://stat.link/1u8ogv

While few empirical evaluations of the effectiveness of COVID-19 related measures have been completed, there is some evidence to suggest that liquidity support, through tax measures and other policy tools, has been effective in limiting bankruptcies in 2020. The domino effect of cascading bankruptcies was one of governments' biggest concerns, but preliminary evidence shows that this has been avoided in many countries. For instance in France, the Central Bank has indicated that domestic corporate bankruptcies declined markedly in 2020 compared to previous years (Banque de France, 2021[4]), suggesting that tax deferrals and other liquidity support measures have been an effective way of immediately enhancing firms' liquidity positions. Analogous evidence was also found in Italy (Giacomelli, Mocetti and Rodano, 2021[5]). However, whilst most businesses have remained solvent up to the beginning of 2020, there is a risk of widespread bankruptcies on the horizon, especially if support is withdrawn too quickly (see Chapter 3).

Recent evidence concerning the effectiveness of stimulus measures has suggested that some measures have had less of an impact than anticipated. In a limited number of countries, recovery-oriented stimulus measures were introduced when significant restrictions on both supply and demand were still in place, severely restricting their effectiveness. In other cases, some stimulus measures may have even been counterproductive from a health perspective, where they encouraged greater social interactions. In the case of VAT rate reductions, there has been some evidence suggesting a relatively limited pass-through from businesses to consumers, with businesses partly using the VAT rate reduction to strengthen their margins. The German Central Bank estimated that only one third of the cut in the German standard VAT rate was passed through to consumer prices in service sectors, noting that many service providers had likely retained most of the VAT cut because containment measures had severely affected their turnover and caused additional costs. However, pass-through was significantly higher in other sectors (Deutsche Bundesbank, 2020[6]).

2.2. Corporate income tax and other business tax measures sought to provide relief to businesses and encourage investment

The majority of CIT measures in advanced and emerging economies have sought to alleviate cash flow difficulties, including through tax payment deferrals, accelerated tax refunds, the reduction of CIT pre-payments and enhanced loss offset provisions. These measures were intended to support businesses experiencing a sharp decline in liquidity, but also to prevent possible ripple effects throughout the economy resulting from companies' difficulties to pay for wages, rent, intermediate goods, and interest on debt. Since mid-2020, when sanitary restrictions began to ease after the first wave of the pandemic, stimulus measures, in particular investment tax incentives, became an increasingly significant component of tax packages in response to the crisis. The timing and scale of tax stimulus measures has nevertheless varied across countries, reflecting in part differences in the timing of virus outbreaks and the speed at which economies began reopening. While the focus of CIT and other business tax measures has very largely been on providing relief and stimulus, a few countries have already introduced or announced reforms aimed at raising tax revenues, including increases in CIT and other business tax rates, as well as base broadening measures.

Figure 2.7. Main CIT measures across groups of countries

Shares of countries reporting tax measures in each group

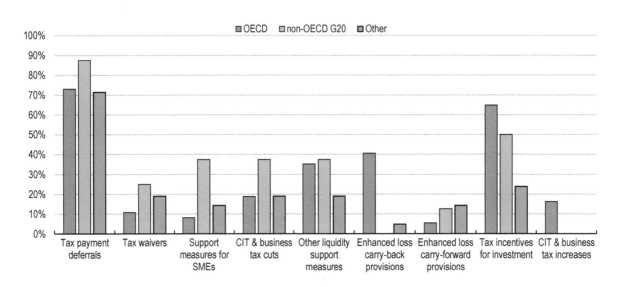

Note: The three groups of countries consist of 37 OECD countries, eight non-OECD G20 countries and 21 other countries and jurisdictions that are members of the OECD/G20 Inclusive Framework.
Source: 2021 OECD Tax Policy Reform Questionnaire.

StatLink 🖳 https://stat.link/1et8h3

Tax payment deferrals and tax filing extensions

The deferral of CIT and other business taxes has been the most common tax measure to enhance business cash flow. Over 75% of the surveyed countries and jurisdictions have introduced deferrals of CIT payments. Many countries accompanied tax deferrals with extensions for the filing of tax returns and other related forms. Some countries even deferred CIT payments by a year (e.g. Japan and Tunisia). Most countries and jurisdictions implemented measures that cover all businesses. Italy also targeted enhanced

CIT and other business tax deferrals at companies severely affected by the crisis (tourism, transport, catering, entertainment, sports and education) and businesses in all sectors with annual revenues below EUR 50 million and experiencing significant drops in turnover. Other countries have exclusively targeted tax deferrals at SMEs and/or simplified regimes from the beginning of the crisis (e.g. Brazil, Korea, New Zealand and Peru). Brazil, for example, deferred payments for taxpayers under the simplified regime (Simples Nacional) for several months in 2020.

Tax deferrals have been extended in many countries as the health crisis has continued (e.g. Austria, Italy, Honduras, Lithuania, Norway, Japan, Peru and Saudi Arabia). During the first outbreak of COVID-19, Peru deferred CIT payments for all SMEs, while in the second wave deferrals were extended only for small firms below a lower turnover threshold located in zones particularly affected by the health crisis.

Several countries have introduced more flexible tax payment plans for businesses. Over one fifth of countries introduced flexible tax repayment plans. In some countries these plans were further eased in the second half of 2020. South Africa, for example, allowed large businesses to apply directly to the tax administration to defer tax payments without incurring penalties if they could prove that they were unable to pay their tax liability as a result of the COVID-19 crisis. Some countries waived, or significantly reduced, penalties on late payments of tax liabilities from previous years (e.g. Ireland, Panama, Peru, Mauritius, Republic of North Macedonia and Saudi Arabia). Nigeria provided interest and penalty relief for businesses that missed their filing deadline. Concurrently, Belgium increased discounts granted to early payments while Greece and Honduras provided tax discounts for payments made on time.

Reduction of tax prepayments

Some countries suspended CIT prepayments during part of 2020 (e.g. Chile, Greece, Indonesia, Luxembourg, Mauritius, Slovenia and Uruguay). Slovenia waived CIT prepayments and prepayments of tax for unincorporated businesses during most of 2020 and Greece applied a similar measure, but only for sectors affected by the pandemic. Chile waived all monthly CIT prepayments during the second quarter of 2020 for all companies and extended this suspension up to September exclusively for businesses experiencing a revenue reduction of at least 30% in the second quarter of the year.

A number of countries reduced tax prepayments for SMEs for a longer period. Portugal waived tax prepayments for cooperatives, micro companies and SMEs in 2021 and Chile reduced monthly payments by half for companies under the SME regime until 2022. New Zealand temporarily increased the threshold for businesses that have to make prepayments to provide relief to small taxpayers.

Some countries and jurisdictions lowered the amount of tax prepayments in anticipation of a drop in businesses' revenue (e.g. Andorra, Honduras and Indonesia). For example, Indonesia reduced monthly CIT instalments for eligible sectors by 30% in the first half of 2020 and by 50% for both the second half of 2020 and the first half of 2021.

Tax refunds

Some countries provided for CIT refunds of advanced payments (e.g. Israel, Portugal). Israel allowed businesses that paid advanced tax payments in 2020 before the start of the COVID-19 crisis, and suffered a drop in activity thereafter to ask for a refund.

Other countries and jurisdictions accelerated the refund of CIT credits (e.g. Barbados, Seychelles, Trinidad and Tobago, and the United States). The United States accelerated the ability of companies to claim a refund for corporate alternative minimum tax credits (which had previously been repealed as part of the Tax Cuts and Jobs Act). The United States also introduced a provision that allowed businesses to retain and access funds that they would otherwise have had to pay to the IRS in payroll taxes to cover the cost of paid leave during 2020.

Tax waivers and rebates

A few countries granted partial or full waivers of CIT liabilities. Singapore granted a CIT rebate of 25% of tax payable (with a cap) in the 2019 fiscal year, and Indonesia granted waivers for various types of withholding taxes until June 2021 for businesses that are involved in the handling of the health crisis. Peru suspended or reduced CIT payments from April to July 2020 depending on the income reduction companies experienced relative to the same month in 2019.

However, most tax waivers applied to other business taxes. Brazil waived the financial transaction tax that it levies on credit transactions for nine months. Hungary and Tunisia both temporarily waived business taxes in the hard-hit travel sector, with Hungary choosing to waive the tourism development contribution and the tourism tax until the state of emergency is lifted and Tunisia waiving travel agencies from the payment of a specific business tax during the first half of 2021. Italy waived stamp duties related to electronic invoices during 2020 and harbour taxes and fees were forgone up to July 2020 for firms operating in the shipping sector. As discussed in section 2.6, some countries waived recurrent taxes on immovable property owned by businesses, which could constitute a large burden for businesses facing sharp losses in revenue.

Tax waivers were targeted at SMEs and the self-employed in some countries. Korea granted a 60% income tax reduction to qualified small-sized enterprises and a 30% income tax reduction for mid-sized enterprises located in particularly affected areas, for the tax year up to 30 June 2020. Italy waived the payment of the regional tax on productive activities (IRAP) for the fiscal year 2019 as well as the 40% prepayment of the IRAP for 2020 for companies and self-employed workers with turnover of up to EUR 250 million, while the second instalment was deferred. Indonesia exempted SMEs from paying the turnover tax up to June 2021. Portugal waived a specific tax levied on businesses that report losses for certain microenterprises and SMEs as of 2021.

CIT and other business tax rate reductions

Very few countries have reduced their standard CIT rate since the start of the crisis, interrupting the long-term trend of declining statutory CIT rates worldwide. The OECD has previously documented the continuous decline in CIT rates over the past 20 years, occurring in both OECD countries (OECD, 2020[2]), but also across African, Asian and Latin American countries (OECD, 2020[7]). This year, however, with very few exceptions, statutory CIT rates have remained stable.

A few countries reduced or accelerated the planned reduction in the standard CIT rate as a response to the crisis. Indonesia reduced its standard CIT rate from 25% to 22% and will further reduce it to 20% as of 2022. In Canada, at the subnational level, Alberta reduced its standard CIT rate from 10% to 8% in July 2020 a year and a half sooner than originally planned, as part of an acceleration of its Job Creation Tax Cut programme.

Other countries reduced their CIT rate in-line with plans made before the COVID-19 crisis hit. India reduced its CIT rate levied on existing domestic companies that do not benefit from any concessional tax regime from 30% to 22%, and to 15% for new domestic manufacturing companies. Colombia permanently reduced its standard CIT rate from 33% in 2019 to 32% in 2020 and 31% in 2021; the rate will be further reduced to 30% from 2022 onwards. Concurrently, Colombia introduced a temporary CIT surcharge on financial institutions, which was set at 4% in 2020 and 3% for 2021 and 2022. Nova Scotia (Canada) reduced its standard CIT from 16% to 14% as of April 2020. Croatia reduced the CIT rate for taxpayers who annually earn revenue up to the HRK 7.5 million from 12% to 10% from 2021 onwards.

Some countries introduced targeted CIT rate reductions and base narrowing measures exclusively for small businesses. Chile temporarily reduced the CIT rate for companies under the SMEs regime (from 25% to 10%) for the fiscal years 2020 to 2022. France increased the turnover threshold for SMEs to benefit from the reduced 15% CIT rate from EUR 7.63 million to EUR 10 million. Albania temporarily granted tax holidays to small businesses as of January 2021. Hungary reduced the small business tax rate from 12% to 11% and increased the eligibility threshold until December 2020. Panama reduced the CIT rates for microenterprises and SMEs applicable from the 2020 fiscal year onwards. Trinidad and Tobago applied a 0% CIT rate for SMEs listed on the local stock exchange (TTSE) for the first five years from the date of listing; a 15% CIT rate will be applied for the next five years, increasing to 30% thereafter. Saskatchewan (Canada) temporarily reduced the small business tax rate. Other Canadian provinces and territories permanently reduced the small business tax rate from 2021 (e.g. Nova Scotia, Northwest Territories, Prince Edward Island, Yukon) although these reductions were not linked to the pandemic and in many cases were announced prior to the onset of the health crisis.

A number of countries targeted the reduction in CIT rates to specific sectors or company types with the aim of encouraging growth. Russia reduced the CIT rate applied to qualified IT and technology companies from 20% to 3% as of January 2021. Argentina reduced the CIT rate (from 25% to 15%) that is applied to businesses engaged in knowledge-related economic activities. Turkey reduced the CIT rate from 22% to 20% for five years for companies that list at least 20% of their shares on the Istanbul Stock Exchange for the first time from January 2021.

Some countries have introduced tax cuts in other business taxes. France introduced a permanent reduction in production taxes for companies in the industrial sector. As part of a long-term plan on banking taxation announced in 2015, the United Kingdom reduced the bank levy rate to 0.1%, which is levied on banks' chargeable equity and liabilities of GBP 20 billion or more as of 2021. The scope of the bank levy was also reduced so that overseas activities of UK headquartered banking groups are no longer subject to the bank levy. The Slovak Republic abolished its bank levy in 2020. To support the transport sector, the Czech Republic reduced the road tax on trucks by 25%. Poland postponed the entry into force of a retail sales tax. Russia abolished the presumptive income tax for certain types of businesses. Thailand reduced the withholding tax rate on certain types of income (e.g. services and professional income, rental income) from 3% to 1.5% from April to September 2020 for payments made through any means and from 5% and 3% to 2% from October 2020 to December 2022 for payments through the e-Withholding Tax system. Indonesia exempted dividend income from taxation if the recipient is a domestic (corporate or individual) taxpayer and the income is reinvested in Indonesia within a set time period (minimum investment requirements apply for dividends received from foreign private companies).

Tax support for employment

Some countries introduced tax incentives to encourage businesses to retain their workers or hire new workers. While many advanced countries channelled support to businesses through job retention schemes (see Box 2.1), partially covering businesses' wage costs to enable them to continue paying (possibly part of) their employees' wages rather than laying them off, some countries have also used tax incentives to support employment. Some countries have sought to boost employment through tax measures such as deferrals and waivers of personal income tax liabilities and in particular of social security contributions (see discussion in Section 2.3). As part of the Coronavirus Aid, Relief, and Economic Security Act (the CARES Act), the United States introduced an Employee Retention Credit for employers of qualified wages paid from March 2020 onwards that can be claimed against employer SSCs. This employee retention credit was further increased from 50% to 70% of qualified wages up to USD 10 000 per quarter until mid-2021 and the cap was increased as of January 2021. The United States has also introduced a tax credit for businesses that provide paid sick leave and paid family and medical leave due to COVID-19 and extended a work opportunity tax credit available to employers for hiring individuals from certain target groups who have consistently faced significant barriers to employment until 2025. Honduras introduced a special deduction for the 2020 fiscal period equivalent to 10% of firms' total payroll, which is granted to companies that do not dismiss or suspend workers during the country's state of emergency.

Some countries have targeted tax incentives for employment on businesses hiring low-income employees, who have been one of the groups to be hit hardest by the crisis. British Columbia (Canada) introduced a tax credit for employers that created new jobs or increased payroll for existing low- or medium-income employees, from the second semester of 2020 onwards. Thailand introduced several enhanced deductions, including a 300% deduction for salary payments to low-wage employees hired by SMEs.

Other liquidity support measures

Some countries introduced tax provisions to, either directly or indirectly, reduce rent expenses for businesses operating in sectors particularly affected by the COVID-19 crisis. Italy introduced tax credits partially covering building rental costs. The measure initially targeted small firms in severely affected sectors and was later expanded to all firm sizes until December 2020. France granted a tax credit to owners who reduced part or the full rent to be due by businesses affected by social distancing measures. The tax credit is calculated as a percentage of the rent that was waived and varies with the number of workers employed by the business. Greece introduced provisions for mandatory or optional rent decreases for businesses since September 2020 while foregoing property owners from paying income tax and social solidarity contribution on these reductions. Similarly, Spain allowed property owners renting out premises to businesses in the tourism, catering and commerce sector to deduct the amount of rent they voluntarily reduced for the months of January to March 2021. Korea also introduced a special tax credit for property owners who voluntarily reduced the rent for small commercial businesses equivalent to half of the rent reduction they provided in the first half of 2020.

Several countries temporarily increased the threshold for low-value asset write-offs to provide liquidity support and incentivise investment. This type of measure was introduced in Australia, Chile, the Czech Republic, Finland and New Zealand. Notably, Australia temporarily increased the instant asset write-off threshold to AUD 150 000 on a per asset basis (up from AUD 30 000) and expanded eligibility to include larger businesses with aggregated annual turnover of less than AUD 500 million (up from AUD 50 million).

Several countries introduced temporary increases to deductions for charitable donations (e.g. China, Croatia, France, Iceland, Indonesia, Nigeria, South Africa and the United States). For example, the United States increased the 10% limitation on deductions for charitable contributions by corporations to 25% of taxable income as well as the limitation on deductions for contributions of food inventory from 15% to 25%. Indonesia allowed deductions for charitable donations linked to the handling of COVID-19.

Other countries have expanded tax concessions to SMEs. For example, Australia expanded access to a range of small business tax concessions by increasing the small business entity turnover threshold for these concessions from AUD 10 million to AUD 50 million.

Some countries have also introduced other changes to corporate tax bases with the aim of providing liquidity support and boosting recovery. The United States temporarily increased the amount of interest expense that businesses are allowed to deduct on their tax returns from 30% to 50% of taxable income (with adjustments) for 2019 and 2020. South Africa postponed the decision to limit net interest expense deductions to 30% of taxable income, as well as a reform that aims at broadening the corporate tax base, to at least January 2022. Norway modified tax provisions of hydropower plants to provide liquidity and facilitate investments as of 2021. Italy reduced the CIT base for taxed activities of non-profit organisations by 50% as of 2021 and allowed merged companies to benefit from deferred tax asset and allowances for corporate equity (ACE) surpluses accrued before the merger.

Enhanced loss offset provisions

Changes to loss-offset provisions have been a particularly important tax policy tool to provide liquidity relief to businesses and support economic recovery. Allowing or expanding loss-carry-back measures, which allow taxpayers to offset their current losses against profits earned in previous fiscal years and lead to refunds of taxes previously paid, can be particularly effective due to the countercyclical effects of these measures. In addition, these measures have the advantage of automatically providing liquidity to lossmaking firms that will typically not benefit from other tax measures such as rate reductions, deferrals or exemptions. Several countries, in particular OECD member countries (38%), have introduced or enhanced existing loss carry-back rules since the outbreak of COVID-19.

Several countries introduced measures allowing loss carry-back for the 2020/21 tax year (e.g. Australia, Austria, Belgium, Czech Republic, New Zealand, Norway, Poland, and the United States). Prior to the COVID-19 crisis, net operating losses (NOL) in the United States were subject to a taxable-income limitation, and could not be carried back to reduce income in a prior tax year. In 2020, the United States introduced a provision that allows NOL arising in a tax year beginning in 2018, 2019, or 2020 to be carried back five years. The provision also temporarily removes the taxable income limitation to allow this loss carry back rule to fully offset income. Australia temporarily allowed qualifying companies to apply losses from the 2019/20, 2020/21, and/ or 2021/22 fiscal years to offset previously taxed profits back to 2018/19.

Several countries eased restrictions and extended existing loss carry back rules. The United Kingdom temporarily extended the loss carry back rule from one to three years for losses up to a cap made in the 2020/21 and 2021/22 fiscal years for both incorporated and unincorporated businesses. Similarly, Singapore temporarily extended its loss carry back rule from one to three years for losses made in the 2019 and 2020 fiscal years, with a cap. Japan temporarily expanded its loss carry back provision, previously available only for small businesses, to medium enterprises up to 2022 (i.e. companies with assets valued at YEN 100 million or less). Germany initially increased its loss carry-back provision to a maximum of EUR 5 million (EUR 10 million for joint assessments) for 2020 and 2021 and recently increased this maximum again to EUR 10 million (double for joint assessments) for the same years. South Africa postponed the decision to restrict the loss offsets to 80% of taxable income until 2022.

Some OECD countries have provided accelerated refunds for losses that have been carried-back (e.g. France, Ireland and the Netherlands). France allowed tax credits resulting from loss carry-back provisions for the 2020 fiscal year to be immediately refunded while Ireland allowed a 50% immediate loss tax refund. The United Kingdom allowed large businesses paying CIT through quarterly instalment payments to submit loss relief claims before the end of their accounting period if they anticipate losses and can sufficiently evidence these. The Netherlands also introduced an early loss offset (Corona tax reserve) that offers companies the possibility to deduct their expected loss in 2020 (instead of a tax assessment) from their profits in 2019. At the same time, the Netherlands aligned its loss carry-back rules with international established practice by restricting the deductibility of liquidation and cessation losses from 2021 and capping loss relief at 50% of the taxable profit (with an amount of up to EUR 1 million being still deductible) from 2022 onwards.

Some countries have eased or extended loss carry-forward provisions as part of their efforts to support economic recovery in the medium-term. China, for example, extended the loss carry-forward period from five to eight years for tax losses incurred in 2020 by companies in sectors severely affected by the pandemic. Portugal extended the carry-forward of losses generated in 2020 or 2021 by large companies from five to twelve years, and Peru extended the carry-forward of losses generated in 2020 from four to five years. The Slovak Republic allowed businesses to carry-forward losses of up to EUR 1 million from 2015 onwards to fully offset the tax base for 2020, helping improve SMEs' liquidity. Uruguay also removed the annual limit on the amount of losses that can be carried forward.

Tax incentives for investment

In addition to corporate tax measures aimed at providing liquidity support, countries also introduced measures to support investment, particularly from mid-2020 onwards. As sanitary restrictions began to ease in many countries and economies started reopening after the first wave of the pandemic, more traditional stimulus policies were introduced with the aim of encouraging new investment and accelerating planned investments. Nevertheless, the timing and scope of stimulus for business investment has varied, with earlier and stronger stimulus through tax incentives tending to come from countries that managed to contain the virus more quickly. Several countries that initially introduced measures to temporarily incentivise investment during 2020 subsequently extended and expanded these measures to 2021 and 2022 (e.g. Italy, with an enhanced tax credit for investment costs related to new, innovative and intangible assets). Other countries introduced new tax incentives for investment as part of broader CIT reforms.

A few countries introduced or enhanced tax provisions linked to COVID-19, including allowances to support businesses adapting their workplaces to new sanitary protocols. The United States, for example, introduced a tax provision that enables businesses, especially in the hospitality industry, to immediately write off costs associated with improving facilities. Italy introduced tax credits that partially cover costs incurred in sanitising firms and upgrading and securing workplaces to enable safer work practices; these tax credits were then prolonged until June 2021. China allowed immediate expensing of investments made to expand the production capacity of businesses engaged in producing key supplies related to COVID-19 protection and containment.

A number of countries have allowed immediate expensing of larger investments to increase cash flow and encourage businesses to bring forward investments (e.g. Australia, the Czech Republic, Mauritius and Norway). Norway temporarily allowed oil and gas companies (taxed under the Petroleum tax regime) to immediately deduct investments made by 2022, including the special deduction (uplift) from the special tax base used for petroleum tax revenue purposes. The Czech Republic allowed immediate depreciation of certain investments, including in office equipment, computers and tools, and also abolished the tax depreciation of intangible assets from 2021 onwards. Australia granted immediate expensing to investments in qualifying assets until June 2022 for business with turnover of less than AUD 5 billion. Mauritius allowed immediate depreciation of investments in new plant and machinery made in the second quarter of 2020. Poland introduced a special fund for investment purposes that allows SMEs to immediately expense the cost of fixed assets.

To encourage investment, some countries have introduced accelerated tax depreciation schemes (e.g. Austria, Belgium, Czech Republic, Iceland, Israel, New Zealand and Singapore). Austria introduced declining balance depreciation (30% per year) as an option for both incorporated and unincorporated businesses as well as accelerated depreciation for buildings as of July 2020. Belgium enhanced its investment deduction percentage, increasing it to 25% for investments in fixed assets made by companies and the self-employed between the second and fourth quarters of 2020. The Czech Republic allowed for tax depreciation over two years for certain assets, including engines, motor vehicles, machines and audio-visual equipment. New Zealand permanently introduced tax depreciation for new and existing industrial and commercial buildings, including hotels and motels at a 2% annual rate (the tax depreciation of industrial and commercial buildings was previously not possible). Singapore provided the option to depreciate for tax purposes the cost of plant and machinery over two years (as opposed to three years), and the cost of renovation and refurbishment over one year (as opposed to three years) in the 2020 and 2021 fiscal years. Peru temporarily increased tax depreciation rates for some types of assets as of 2021 and allowed travel agencies, hotels, restaurants and related services to depreciate their buildings and constructions at a 20% rate in 2021 and 2022.

Several countries enhanced deductions to support investment in new machinery and equipment (e.g. Germany, Portugal, Sweden, Trinidad and Tobago and the United Kingdom). The United Kingdom announced a 130% capital allowance deduction for qualifying new main rate plant and machinery investments, and a 50% first-year deduction for qualifying special rate (long-life) assets from April 2021 until March 2023. Germany modified and expanded the eligibility criteria for enhanced and accelerated tax depreciation allowances for movable assets, including machinery, so that not only start-ups but also SMEs can benefit from these incentives as of 2021. Portugal introduced a temporary special investment tax credit of up to 20% of investment expenses (up to EUR 5 million) in both tangible and intangible assets made between July 2020 and June 2021. The tax credit is limited to 70% of CIT liability but may be carried forward for five years. Sweden announced an Investment Tax Incentive that will enter into force in 2022.

Several countries have introduced incentives targeted at environmentally friendly investments (e.g. Denmark, France, Iceland, Spain and the United States). Spain allowed businesses to choose the speed of tax depreciation for investments made until June 2021 in the electric, sustainable or connected mobility value chain. Italy introduced in 2020 a tax credit up to 110% of the costs incurred for green transition investments, which was further extended to 2021 and 2022. The United States modified and made permanent the energy efficient commercial buildings deduction as of 2021. Denmark temporarily introduced an enhanced tax depreciation provision to promote investment in certain green technologies, while France introduced a tax credit for energy-saving renovation works in SMEs' buildings as well as for the installation of equipment to recharge electric vehicles.

Some countries increased the generosity of their tax subsidies targeted at specific sectors. Spain enhanced tax credits for film production (on a permanent basis) and technological innovation in the automotive sector to support investment in this sector during 2020/2021. Thailand introduced enhanced deductions for investments in the hospitality sector during 2020. Italy introduced enhanced tax credits that partially cover the costs of restructuring touristic buildings in 2020 and 2021. Quebec (Canada) introduced a new 30% synergy capital tax credit, subject to an annual cap of CAN 225 000, granted to corporations that buy shares of a qualified corporation in the life sciences, manufacturing or processing, green technologies, artificial intelligence or information technologies sectors as of January 2021.

Some countries introduced or expanded tax incentives that are targeted at specific regions. Mexico extended the tax credits targeted at taxpayers from the northern border region that were scheduled to end in 2020 to 2024 (the tax credit is equivalent to one third of their income tax liability), and also extended the scope to the southern border region. In addition, these tax credits have now become available to qualified businesses in the southern border region. Ontario (Canada) implemented a new refundable tax credit, with a cap of CAN 500 000, for capital investments made by Canadian-controlled private corporations in commercial and industrial buildings in specified regions of the province.

Several countries increased the generosity of tax provisions targeted at R&D and intellectual property. In 2020 several countries announced or introduced new R&D tax incentives or increased the generosity of existing R&D tax relief provisions (e.g. Australia, China, Finland, Germany, Indonesia, Italy, Mauritius and Turkey). Germany expanded its tax credits for companies that carry out specific research by increasing the maximum level of R&D tax support that can be received over a six-year period. Indonesia introduced a 300% deduction of the actual R&D costs incurred. In China, the 175% super deduction for R&D expenses, which was to expire in 2020, was extended and raised to 200% for manufacturing firms. Italy introduced a new tax credit for R&D and investment in innovative technology (available until 2022) and strengthened the existing R&D tax credit for firms operating in the Mezzogiorno region. Quebec (Canada) introduced a deduction for the commercialisation of innovations, which enables a corporation that commercialises a qualified intellectual property asset developed in Quebec to benefit from an effective tax rate of 2% on the qualified portion of its taxable income attributable to that qualified intellectual property asset (compared to the standard provincial CIT rate of 11.5%). Turkey extended existing R&D tax incentives that were about to end in 2021 to 2028.

Some countries have increased the generosity of specific tax incentives regimes (in many cases with a strong focus on the IT sector) as an attempt to attract FDI. Korea expanded its tax incentives for companies that relocate to Korea. This includes a CIT holiday for the first 5 to 7 years if the company relocates its activity outside the Seoul Metropolitan area and 3 to 5 years if it relocates its activity inside the Seoul Metropolitan area. China granted tax holidays to companies producing integrated circuit chips of up to 10 years (benefits vary with the size of the chips produced) from 2021 onwards. Italy confirmed its project to implement special economic zones (SEZs) in some harbour areas in Southern regions. Lithuania introduced a tax holiday of up to 20 years for companies undertaking large investment projects contracted from 2021 to 2025 under the condition that at least 75 per cent of income is related to data processing, web server services and related activities or to manufacturing. Indonesia expanded the eligibility criteria for industries to qualify as so-called pioneers and benefit from a tax holiday for investment projects of at least IDR 100 billion. India extended a tax scheme for start-ups registered between 2016 and 2021 by one more year (i.e. eligible start-ups registered until March 2022). Argentina introduced a specific regime that aims at stimulating knowledge-related economic activities. The regime benefits from a reduced CIT rate and grants a tax credit that amounts to 70% of employer SSCs while other tax incentives vary with firm size.

CIT and other business tax increases

Some countries have already introduced or announced corporate and business tax increases, with the objective of raising revenue. As discussed in Chapter 1, the crisis will in many countries lead to a significant drop in tax revenue. In addition to revenue declines, the costs of fiscal packages to support businesses and households during (partial) lockdowns and measures to incentivise economic recovery together with the increase in public spending to mitigate health damages will lead to deteriorating budget balances. In this context, a few countries have introduced or announced measures aimed at raising revenue in the future.

A few countries announced CIT rate increases in the medium term or reversed planned tax cuts. The United Kingdom announced an increase in the CIT rate from 19% to 25% as of April 2023. The rate will be tapered so that only businesses with profits of more than GBP 250 000 will be taxed at the full 25% rate, while companies with profits of less than GBP 50 000 will remain at 19%. In addition, the United Kingdom announced the increase in the Diverted Profits Tax from 25% to 31% as of April 2023 so that it remains a deterrent against diverting profits out of the United Kingdom in the context of the announced future CIT rate increases. The Netherlands reversed the intended decrease of the higher CIT rate to 21.7%, maintaining the rate at 25%, while increasing the higher tax bracket from EUR 200 000 to EUR 245 000 in 2021 and EUR 395 000 in 2022.

Some countries increased other business taxes or introduced tax base broadening measures. Hungary temporarily introduced a one-off tax on banks and credit institutions and a special retail tax during the first half of 2020. France introduced a temporary tax on private healthcare providers to be levied in 2021. The Netherlands increased the rate of the Dutch innovation box regime from 7% to 9% as of 2021. As part of the 2018-2023 coalition agreement, Luxembourg introduced a 20% withholding tax on income derived from real estate located in Luxembourg by certain Luxembourg investment funds from 2021 onwards. Sweden announced a new tax on the financial sector that will be in force in 2023. The Slovak Republic reduced the threshold (from EUR 100 000 to 49 790) for which micro-taxpayers benefit from a 15% CIT reduced rate from 2021 onwards.

International tax measures

Countries continue to improve their CIT systems' robustness against base erosion and profit shifting (BEPS), thereby also increasing the stability of public finances. Portugal introduced new provisions to disallow tax deductions resulting from hybrid mismatches and expanded the definition of permanent establishment to combat the tax-driven fragmentation of multinational activities carried out in

Portugal. Poland implemented an EU Council Directive (2017/952) to prevent hybrid mismatches. The Netherlands introduced a stricter limitation of interest deductions as part of the implementation of the EU's Anti-Tax Avoidance Directive 1 (ATAD1) as of 2021. Spain reduced the full exemption of dividends and capital gains derived from resident and non-resident companies to 95% with certain exclusions.

Norway is introducing a differentiated withholding tax of 15% on interest and royalties, similar to the approach that was implemented in the Netherlands earlier this year. To prevent profit shifting to low-tax jurisdictions through incorrect pricing of transactions between enterprises in the same group, a 15% withholding tax is introduced on the payment of interest, royalties and rent on certain physical assets from enterprises with activities in Norway to associated enterprises in low-tax jurisdictions. The changes will enter into effect on 1 July 2021.

As the discussions on a global consensus to address the tax challenges arising from the digitalisation of the economy are ongoing, some countries have resorted to unilateral tax measures. The United Kingdom and Spain introduced digital services taxes as of 2021. Indonesia delayed the introduction of an income tax or Electronic Transaction Tax (ETT) on offshore digital businesses that have a significant economic presence in Indonesia until consensus-based solution is reached.

2.3. Personal income taxes and social security contributions were used to provide relief to households and employers, but several countries also raised tax rates on high earners

Many countries introduced PIT and SSC relief measures to support households and employers. Some countries also introduced permanent or open-ended tax reductions. Self-employed workers were among those hit hardest by the crisis and a number of countries responded by introducing targeted tax relief for the self-employed. Overall, tax payment deferrals and filing extensions continue to be the most common short-term labour tax measures, followed by increased tax allowances and SSCs waivers. Some countries also increased their incentives for philanthropic donations. In the second half of 2020 and early 2021, some OECD and G20 countries introduced tax increases on high-income earners, including increases in top PIT rates.

Figure 2.8. Main PIT and SSC measures across groups of countries

Shares of countries reporting tax measures in each group

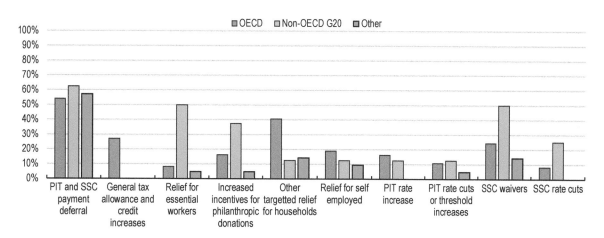

Note: The three groups of countries consist of 37 OECD countries, eight non-OECD G20 countries and 21 other countries and jurisdictions that are members of the OECD/G20 Inclusive Framework. Relief for self-employed includes loss carry-back provisions, increased tax allowances and credits, and rate cuts.
Source: 2021 OECD Tax Policy Reform Questionnaire.

StatLink ⟐ https://stat.link/e6m1sq

Tax payment deferrals and other PIT administration measures

The most common type of measure related to labour taxes across countries has been the deferral of PIT and SSCs payments (e.g. Israel, Italy, Latvia, Lithuania, Nigeria, Peru, Slovenia, Spain, and Sweden). While the majority of countries deferred all tax liabilities, others (e.g. Spain) capped the amount that could be deferred. After deferring taxes in the first half of 2020 as an emergency response to the first wave of the pandemic, many countries extended the number of months that tax payments could be deferred in the second half of 2020. Furthermore, some countries have waived interest or fees on late labour tax payments. For self-employed workers, PIT deferrals and waived advance payments were common relief measures in a number of countries and jurisdictions (e.g. Latvia, Italy, Slovenia, Barbados, Poland, Russia, and the United States). Other measures for the self-employed also included filling extensions (e.g. Nigeria).

In addition to deferrals, several countries have also continued to extend their tax filing deadlines (e.g. Barbados, Mexico, India, Luxembourg, Thailand, Tunisia, Turkey, Nigeria and the United States). The United States extended the tax filing deadline for individuals both for the 2020 and the 2021 filing season. Although most deferrals and extensions have been applied broadly, some countries implemented more targeted deferrals and extensions for taxpayers disproportionately affected by the COVID-19 crisis (e.g. Lithuania and Peru). Other measures include accelerated payments of tax refunds, including, for example, refunds of excess PIT payments (e.g. Chile, Barbados, South Africa, and Israel), as well as flexible arrangements for tax debt repayments.

To strengthen cash flow for self-employed workers, some countries accelerated their PIT refunds (e.g. Israel and Chile). Chile, for example, refunded the advanced payments or PIT withholdings. Other countries (e.g. the Slovak Republic) increased the tax liability threshold that determines the obligation to pay quarterly advanced payments.

Extended or new personal income tax allowances and credits

Many countries introduced short-term PIT relief measures in the first half of 2020, and extended or expanded them afterwards. Countries have indicated that the most common rationale for these reforms was to provide tax relief and support to those hit hardest by the crisis, enhance households' cash flow, increase purchasing power, and stimulate demand and employment. The level of targeting of PIT relief provisions varied across countries. Some countries implemented broad measures, some more targeted measures for those hit hardest by the pandemic to support families, essential workers, and low-income households (e.g. New Zealand and Nigeria), and others a combination of broadly available and more targeted measures (e.g. Germany and Canada).

Measures available to all or most taxpayers included increased standard tax allowances (e.g. Canada, Germany, Lithuania, and United Kingdom) and general tax credits (e.g. Czech Republic, Finland, Italy, Luxembourg, Netherlands, and Sweden). Germany, for example, increased its basic personal allowance by EUR 336 (from EUR 9 408 to EUR 9 744) as of 1 January 2021, which is in line with increases in the past. Germany also increased its exemption threshold for non-cash benefits. Lithuania, increased its basic personal allowance by EUR 50 (from EUR 350 to EUR 400) for 2020 in response to the COVID-19 crisis. The United Kingdom introduced an inflationary increase of their basic personal allowance. The Czech Republic increased its tax credits for all employees and self-employed workers. The Netherlands increased its general tax credit, employed persons tax credit, and old age tax credit from 2021, while decreasing the tax credit for combining work and childcare. Italy introduced a non-refundable tax credit[1] in the first half of 2020 and made it permanent in the second half of 2020. As part of a long term plan, Prince Edward Island (Canada) increased its basic personal income tax allowance by CAD 500 to a new threshold of CAD 10 500, as of 1 January 2021.

On the other hand, some countries have introduced measures that are targeted at individual taxpayers hit hardest by the pandemic, including families with children, essential workers, and low-income households (e.g. Canada, New Zealand, and Nigeria). Such measures include increased income tax allowances for households with children (e.g. Germany, Estonia), for vulnerable individuals (e.g. Sweden and Germany), and earned income tax credits for low-income households.

One approach to providing PIT relief to low-income households was through earned income tax credits. Luxembourg increased its existing tax credit for employees, self-employed and pensioners from EUR 600 to EUR 696. Finland increased the earned income tax credit to further reduce the tax burden on labour. Additionally, some non-OECD or G20 countries provided targeted tax support to low-income households by exempting their income from tax altogether. Nigeria, for example, temporarily exempted minimum wage earners from PIT.

Countries that provided PIT relief to support families did so through targeted tax allowances and child credits. Germany, Estonia, and the United States increased income tax allowances for households with children. Germany, for example, permanently increased its single-parent income tax allowance[2] from EUR 1 908 to EUR 4 008 per year, and increased the basic allowance for children from EUR 7 812 to EUR 8 388. Estonia introduced a supplementary basic allowance for a third child. Belgium increased the maximum amount of child care expenses eligible for an already existing tax credit. The United States temporarily increased the amount of its child tax credit for low- and middle-income taxpayers up to USD 3 600 per young child and up to USD 3 000 for older children for 2021. Furthermore, the United States made the credit fully refundable and payable in advance, and implemented look-back provisions allowing households to use their 2019 income to compute their child credits.

Some countries introduced new tax exemptions for extraordinary income related to essential work. Argentina, China, Germany, Russia, Austria, Indonesia, Thailand, and the United States introduced tax exemptions for bonuses or compensation received by essential and medical workers. In Germany, the measure was originally intended to be in force until 31 December 2020, but was recently extended to 30 June 2021. Argentina introduced a tax exemption for front line workers in sectors effected by COVID-19 (health, hygiene, security, and fire and rescue). Indonesia temporarily applied a 0% PIT rate for additional income received from government by health sector workers dealing with COVID-19. Thailand provided tax exemptions for income received by healthcare and medical workers as compensation for the risk associated with COVID-19 in the 2020 tax year.

Some countries provided tax relief to the elderly (e.g. Sweden, Canada, Honduras and Thailand). Sweden, for instance, increased its standard tax allowance for elderly people. Ontario (Canada) implemented the temporary Seniors' Home Safety Tax Credit, worth 25% of up to CAD 10 000 in eligible expenses for a senior's principal residence in the province. Manitoba (Canada) implemented the Seniors Economic Recovery Credit, which provides a CAD 200 one-time, refundable tax credit to Manitoba seniors facing additional costs due to the COVID-19 pandemic such as grocery deliveries and technology purchases to stay connected to relatives. Honduras granted taxpayers over 65 a deduction of HNL 80 000. Thailand increased its tax allowance for health insurance premiums from THB 15 000 to THB 25 000.

Some countries implemented targeted tax relief for students and educators to support employment and enhance skills (Lithuania, Netherlands, and United States). Lithuania, for example, expanded the PIT allowance for studies in 2020 and subsequent years. The Netherlands broadened its exemption for study and training costs to also include compensation for study or training costs to laid-off employees. The United States implemented educator expense deduction rules, which permit eligible educators[3] to deduct up to USD 250 of qualifying expenses per year (USD 500 if married, filing jointly and both spouses are eligible educators, but not more than USD 250 each).

A number of countries provided targeted tax relief for teleworking expenses (e.g. Canada, Germany, New Zealand, and Sweden). Sweden, for example, introduced a temporary tax credit for earned income to compensate for increased work related costs due to COVID-19. To simplify the process for both taxpayers and businesses, Canada allowed employees who worked from home in 2020 due to COVID-19 to claim up to CAD 400 without the need to track detailed expenses. Some countries (e.g. Croatia) temporarily exempted work related (fringe) benefits that are associated with COVID-19, such as covered costs for laboratory tests and vaccines.

Some countries and jurisdictions extended tax allowances and credits to support the self-employed (e.g. Germany, Italy, Macau, Russia, and Uruguay). Germany, for example, temporarily increased its tax allowances for unincorporated businesses and self-employed, including, among others, depreciation allowances for movable assets, allowances for bonus payments, and investment allowances. In Russia, self-employed individuals from the age of 16 received an income tax exemption of the amount of a minimum monthly salary (RUB 12 130). Italy provided a tax credit for rent payments of the self-employed. To support the tourism sector, Uruguay temporarily (until April 2021) exempted from tax the rental income from property that is rented out to tourists.

Countries also introduced loss carry-back provisions for the self-employed (Belgium, Germany, Czech Republic, Poland, and Ireland). Germany, for example, temporarily increased its loss carry-back provision to a maximum of EUR 5 million (or EUR 10 million in the case of joint assessments) for 2020 and 2021. Ireland introduced a new once-off income tax relief loss carry-back provision capped at EUR 25 000 for self-employed individuals carrying on a trade or profession who were profitable in 2019, but as a result of the COVID-19 pandemic, incurred losses in the 2020 tax year.

Other measures were targeted at landlords (e.g. France, Korea, Luxembourg, and Spain). Three countries (France, Luxembourg and Spain) reported tax relief for landlords that reduced their rents for companies. Luxembourg introduced a tax allowance twice the amount of the reduction granted to the business and limited to EUR 15 000. In Spain, the amount that landlords voluntarily reduced their rent (for companies and individuals) is considered a deductible expense for the months of January to March 2021. France and Korea introduced similar measures in the form of a tax credit.

Some countries have targeted measures at shareholders of companies hit hard by the crisis. The Netherlands, for instance, offered major shareholders the possibility to lower their taxable income if their companies experienced a decrease in revenue caused by COVID-19.

Four countries (Canada, Italy, Ireland, and Thailand), introduced tax credits or deductions to subsidise or simply incentivise consumption and indirectly support businesses. Ireland introduced a temporary tax credit, called the Stay and Spend Incentive, aimed at subsidising the consumption of qualifying food and accommodation services. The 20% tax credit is capped at EUR 125, or EUR 250 for a jointly assessed couple. Taxpayers can claim the Stay and Spend credit for qualifying expenditure incurred between 1 October 2020 and 30 April 2021. Thailand, on the other hand, provided a PIT deduction of up to THB 30 000 (about EUR 840) for purchasing products and services subject to the 7% VAT rate from 23 October 2020 to 31 December 2020. Canada implemented a one-time special payment by early May 2020 through their Goods and Services Tax Credit (GSTC), thereby doubling the annual GSTC amount for the 2019-20 tax year. Korea temporarily increased the deduction rate applied to credit card expenditures from March to July 2020. Italy temporarily provided tourism vouchers in the form of a tax credit between EUR 150 and EUR 500 granted to households with income lower than EUR 40 000.[4] In addition, Italy introduced other tax measures in response to the crisis, including a transferable tax credit of up to 110% for the renovation of domestic buildings if it improves energy efficiency and seismic resilience.

A number of countries and jurisdictions have also expanded their preferential tax treatment of charitable contributions in general (e.g. Belgium, Indonesia, Macau, Spain, Slovenia and the United States) or specifically for causes related to COVID-19 (e.g., China, Italy, Poland and South Africa). The United States temporarily increased the charitable contributions PIT deduction and allowed taxpayers who do not itemise, an above-the-line charitable deduction of up to USD 300 (USD 600 for married couples) for 2021. Belgium increased its tax credit for donations from private individuals from 45% to 60%. China and Italy, on the other hand, expanded their charitable deduction for donations related to COVID-19. In South

Africa, the tax-deductible limit for donations (currently 10% of taxable income) was increased by an additional 10% for donations to the Solidarity Fund during the 2020/21 tax year.

PIT rate changes and tax threshold changes

PIT rate cuts or threshold increases were less common but have been implemented in a number of countries (e.g. Australia, Austria, Croatia, Germany, the Netherlands, and South Africa). Both Australia and Croatia had planned their PIT rate cuts before the COVID-19 crisis. In Australia, the reforms were introduced as part of the second stage of the Australian Personal Income Tax Plan, which was brought forward by two years to provide immediate tax relief to individuals and support the economic recovery by boosting consumption during the COVID-19 crisis. The second stage increased the top threshold of the 19% bracket from AUD 37 000 to AUD 45 000 and the top threshold of the 32.5% bracket from AUD 90 000 to AUD 120 000. In addition, the changes retained the low- and middle-income tax offset (LMITO) for 2020-2021 and increased the low income tax offset (LITO). Croatia reduced its PIT rates from 24% to 20% and from 36% to 30% for its two income brackets of below and above HRK 360 000 (EUR 49 000) respectively. Furthermore, the government also reduced the tax rate on dividends from 12% to 10%. These measures were part of a structural reform that was announced prior to the COVID-19 crisis. Austria reduced the bottom PIT rate from 25% to 20% and extended the top PIT rate of 55% (originally set to expire in 2020) until 2025 for income above EUR 1 million. South Africa increased its PIT brackets, and the primary, secondary and tertiary rebates[5] by 5.2% for 2020/21 (which is above expected inflation of 4.4%). The Netherlands, will marginally decrease its PIT rate in 2022, 2023 and 2024 for the first PIT bracket. The Netherlands increased the income tax rate levied on the presumptive return on the value of household savings to 31% in combination with an increase of the tax free threshold to EUR 50 000 (currently EUR 30 846), which is expected to decrease tax revenues. Furthermore, as was proposed in 2019, Germany abolished its solidarity tax at the beginning of 2021 for around 90% of those who paid it and a further 6.5% will pay less.

To raise revenue, some countries have implemented tax rate increases on high-income households. British Columbia (Canada), Colombia, Korea, New Zealand, and Spain all introduced a new top PIT bracket with rates of 20.5%, 39%, 45%, 39%, and 45.5% respectively. The new top PIT rates apply to income over CAD 200 000 in British Columbia (Canada), KRW 1 billion in Korea, NZD 180 000 in New Zealand, and EUR 300 000 in Spain. Additionally, Spain introduced other revenue raising measures increasing the tax burden on high-income households, including a new top tax bracket for income from savings and lower tax deduction ceiling for annual pension contributions. The revenue raised as a result of the rate increase is intended to be invested in the health system. Mauritius implemented a Solidarity Levy through which every individual whose taxable income exceeds MUR 3 million per tax year, is liable to pay a 25% solidarity tax capped at 10% of taxable income. Colombia applies the same PIT rate schedule to labour, and pension income as opposed to the previous system in which pension income was taxed separately (different rates are applied to dividend income and occasional gains). A very generous monthly pension exemption applies.

Two countries (Russia and the Czech Republic) moved from a flat to a progressive PIT system. Russia did so by increasing its PIT rate from 13% to 15% for certain types of income of individuals earning income exceeding RUB 5 million. The Czech Republic introduced a top PIT rate of 23% which applies to income exceeding the social security payment cap (in 2021 that threshold was CZK 1 701 168) and replaces the solidarity tax. Income below that threshold is subject to the 15% rate.

Rate reductions limited to self-employed workers have been rare. Only the Slovak Republic changed its tax rate for the self-employed with income below EUR 49 790 from 21% to 15%. Poland broadened the group of taxpayers who can choose a flat-rate income tax and additionally lowered the rate for liberal professions. The categories now include the self-employed in the tourism sector, revenues from leases of property, and services for the purpose of research and development activity. To further lower the administrative burden on self-employed workers, the Czech Republic provided those self-employed that are registered for the VAT the possibility of a single flat rate payment covering PIT, SSCs and health insurance premiums.

Social Security Contributions (SSCs)

As with the PIT and other taxes, most countries deferred SSCs payments and extended filing deadlines (e.g. Argentina, Brazil, Italy, Jersey, Russia, and the United States). The United States has allowed employers and self-employed individuals to defer payment of the employer share of the Social Security tax. Employers generally are responsible for paying a 6.2% Social Security tax on employee wages.

About 25% of OECD and G20 countries and 14% of other jurisdictions surveyed introduced time-bound and typically targeted SSC waivers (e.g. Argentina, Canada, China, France, Korea, Estonia, Hungary, Italy, Jersey, Poland, Slovenia, Sweden, Macau, Russia, South Africa, and Uruguay). Some countries (e.g. France, Hungary, Italy, Poland, and Uruguay) targeted the SSCs waiver to employers and employees in sectors or regions that were severely affected by the crisis (e.g. tourism, restaurants, cultural services, farmers); other countries (e.g. Italy and Slovenia) targeted employees in vulnerable situations (unemployed, part-time), and a few jurisdictions (e.g. Estonia, Sweden, and Jersey) applied the waivers more universally. Italy also partially waived SSCs for firms hiring workers on permanent contracts and firms renouncing job retention schemes. Some countries implemented SSC rate reductions (e.g. China, Hungary, Iceland, Russia, and Sweden). Hungary, for example, cut employers' SSCs by two percentage points from 17.5% to 15.5% from 1 July 2020.

2.4. Value added tax measures and other consumption tax changes were primarily aimed at easing liquidity pressures on businesses and encouraging consumption

The focus of VAT/GST measures introduced in 2020 and early 2021 has been on reducing compliance costs (e.g. tax filing and reporting extensions) and easing liquidity pressures for businesses (e.g. VAT payment deferrals, accelerated VAT refunds). Some of these measures actually enhance the functioning of VAT systems and ensure that VAT does not weigh on businesses. VAT and import duty relief was also a key part of countries' efforts to ease access to essential medical supplies and services. As sanitary restrictions began to ease and economies started reopening after the first wave of the pandemic, a number of countries introduced temporary VAT/GST rate reductions, generally targeted at specific sectors, as a way to encourage demand and support businesses in severely affected sectors. Many of these temporary rate reductions were extended, as new lockdowns and containment measures were introduced. VAT/GST rate reductions were largely concentrated in OECD countries. On the other hand, excise duties on harmful consumption, in particular on tobacco products, were raised in a number of countries to raise revenue and encourage healthier behaviours.

Figure 2.9. Main VAT/GST measures across groups of countries

Shares of countries reporting tax measures in each group

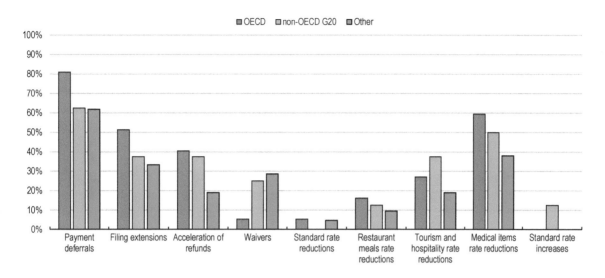

Note: The three groups of countries consist of 37 OECD countries, eight non-OECD G20 countries and 21 other countries and jurisdictions that are members of the OECD/G20 Inclusive Framework.
Source: 2021 OECD Tax Policy Reform Questionnaire

StatLink ᴀ鬥➡ https://stat.link/dv12zg

Tax payment deferrals

Measures to defer the payment of VAT have played a critical role in supporting business cash flow. VAT can often be due before businesses have effectively received payments from their customers (e.g. at the time of invoicing). With the risk of payment delays and defaults rising notably during the pandemic, businesses have faced growing pressure to pre-finance VAT on their sales that they have not, and may never receive, from their customers. Given the typically short VAT filing and payment obligations (monthly or quarterly), the pressure on businesses to pre-finance potentially considerable amounts of VAT that they have not received from their customers can build up very quickly. VAT deferrals can therefore play a significant role in reducing business cash flow pressures. In addition to providing temporary relief from the burden of having to pre-finance VAT on unpaid invoices, these measures can be an efficient way of providing financial support to businesses by allowing them to deploy any VAT received temporarily as working capital (OECD, 2020[8]). Over the last year, VAT deferrals have been introduced in all but two OECD and G20 countries and in approximately 65% of other surveyed jurisdictions. These measures have been extended in almost all countries outside of Asia, and in most cases have become more discretionary as countries increased targeting towards those most in need. The vast majority of countries have complemented VAT payment deferrals with a suspension or reduction of penalties and/or interest charges that normally apply for late tax payments.

The design of VAT deferrals has varied somewhat across countries. Most countries have required businesses to apply for the relief and/or to prove a link with the COVID-19 crisis, but some have applied these measures automatically. Several countries made these measures available to all businesses, but most have limited them to certain sectors (e.g. tourism, retail, entertainment and hospitality) or have targeted SMEs or self-employed businesses (OECD, 2020[9]). More recently, some countries have offered businesses flexibility to opt for partial deferral or to negotiate a flexible payment plan with their tax administration (e.g. Slovenia and the United Kingdom).

Acceleration of VAT refunds

Eighteen OECD and G20 countries and four of the other countries surveyed have taken measures to accelerate and/or to enhance the processing of excess input VAT refund claims. Enhancing the refunding of excess VAT credits is a key measure to improve business cash flow. While output VAT is falling for many businesses as a result of declining sales, the input VAT on fixed costs and other business purchases keeps accruing. These may be significant as many businesses may face payment obligations under longer-term contracts, e.g. for key functions that they may have outsourced to third-party contractors. This may lead to growing amounts of excess input VAT credits, i.e. VAT incurred on costs and investment that cannot be credited against VAT collected on sales. This may generate spill-over effects, with businesses potentially defaulting on their invoices to avoid the growing cost of non-refunded VAT, and defaults rippling through supply chains (OECD, 2020[8]). Several countries, including for instance Canada, Chile, Finland, Indonesia, Saudi Arabia, South Africa, Switzerland, and Thailand, have therefore implemented measures to facilitate and/or accelerate excess-VAT refund procedures. The conditions for facilitated and/or accelerated VAT refunds may differ across countries, with some only allowing these measures to be applied for VAT refund claims below a certain value threshold, others permitting only certain types of businesses to be eligible for accelerated refunds. In some instances in non-OECD countries, eligibility for accelerated VAT refunds is restricted to taxpayers with good tax compliance records.

Bad debt relief regimes

A relatively limited number of tax authorities have sought to lessen liquidity pressures by providing relief to companies who have accumulated bad debts as a result of unpaid invoices from struggling and insolvent firms. Bad debt relief regimes allow businesses to claim relief from the VAT on the supplies for which they have not been paid. Most VAT systems provide for such relief under relatively strict conditions. Some countries have temporarily relaxed these conditions to further alleviate cash flow pressure for businesses (OECD, 2020[8]). Estonia, Hungary, Poland and Sweden, for example, reduced the administrative requirements to obtain tax relief on bad debts and/or reduced the length of time for which the debt must have remained unpaid. Some countries have stressed the need to carefully consider interactions between bad debt relief and VAT payment deferrals, given that VAT bad debt relief should only be available to the extent that VAT on unpaid supplies has been paid to tax authorities.

Tax filing extensions and other simplification measures

Deadline extensions for filling VAT returns and other reporting obligations have been introduced in a number of countries. Measures to facilitate VAT compliance play an important role given the volume and frequency of filing and reporting requirements associated with the operation of a VAT (including returns, invoices or sales listings). Around 40% of all countries who responded to the questionnaire have extended deadlines for the filing of VAT returns and related forms, along with the waiver of penalties for late filing. Some tax authorities have introduced further reporting simplifications, such as allowing VAT liabilities to be computed on a "best estimate" basis. It should be mentioned, however, that tax authorities have typically made the extension of filing and reporting deadlines available only on request and/or in limited cases, in light of the possible consequences of these measures for both taxpayers and tax administrations. VAT returns are an important source of information to monitor the economic impact of COVID-19, to identify which businesses and/or sectors require additional assistance and to support a proper management of compliance risks and tax debts. VAT returns may also be used to provide government support. For businesses, the filing of VAT returns is generally required to claim refunds of excess VAT credits, which highlights the importance of making filing extensions optional, otherwise it could increase businesses' cash flow pressures rather than reduce them (OECD, 2020[8]).

Less common measures to reduce compliance costs have included raising VAT registration thresholds or amending simplified regimes for small businesses. In Korea, the revenue threshold to qualify as a simplified taxable person was raised from KRW 30 million to KRW 48 million and simplified taxable persons were made exempt from VAT payment obligations until the end of 2020. Albania permanently increased its VAT registration threshold fivefold. In Croatia, the eligibility threshold for the application of the VAT cash accounting scheme, which allows businesses to account for the VAT on their sales on the basis of the payments they receive rather than on the invoices they issue, was doubled.

Several countries have temporarily suspended audits and other enforcement and/or recovery actions (e.g. Canada, Greece, Italy, Israel, the United States and many non-OECD countries) to limit the additional stress and diversion of resources and time that these actions may cause during the COVID-19 crisis and to limit-face-to-face interaction. Cases involving fraud or businesses with a high-risk profile have typically been excluded from these measures.

Some countries have delayed planned reforms in order to avoid increases in compliance costs. Delays of reforms have included, among others, the postponement of real-time reporting requirements and delays in the introduction of new e-invoicing rules, e-filing requirements and formats and of electronic cash registers (e.g. Hungary, Italy, and Poland).

VAT/GST rate changes

As countries emerged from the first wave of the pandemic, almost half of all OECD and G20 governments temporarily reduced VAT rates applied to sectors particularly affected by the pandemic. As illustrated in Table 2.2, the tourism and hospitality sector received the most widespread support with 13 OECD and G20 countries temporarily reducing VAT rates applied by the sector, as did restaurant services (eight countries) and the cultural and sports sectors (nine countries). A limited number of the non-OECD/G20 countries surveyed also introduced temporary VAT reductions in specific sectors (e.g. Bulgaria, Croatia, Paraguay, Uruguay). In most instances, targeted reduced VAT rates were initially introduced for periods of between three to six months, but were subsequently extended in a large number of cases for at least a further six months (or while wider restrictions remain in place), most commonly in the hospitality, restaurants and tourism sectors. Notably, extensions to temporary VAT rate reductions were less common in non-OECD countries.

A few countries temporarily reduced their standard VAT rates and general reduced VAT/GST rates. In Germany and Ireland, the standard VAT rate was cut for a period of six months, from 19% to 16% until the end of 2020, and from 23% to 21% until the end of February 2021, respectively. Thailand extended its 3 percentage point reduction in the standard VAT rate to 7% until 30 September 2021. Germany also lowered its general reduced rate from 7% to 5% during the second half of 2020, as did Norway, which extended the time period during which the reduced rate VAT applying to hotels, tourism, cultural admissions and public transport is halved (from 12% to 6%) by a further eight months to June 2021. The exception was Saudi Arabia, where the standard VAT rate was raised from 5% to 15% in July 2020, in part to compensate for the revenue decline resulting from lower oil prices.

Italy and Poland delayed planned changes to their VAT/GST rates. Italy abolished VAT safeguard clauses previously providing for an increase in its standard VAT rate from 22% to 25%, having already delayed the rise for 2019 and 2020. The rise in the reduced rate of 10% to 12%, also set for January 2021, did not take place either. Conversely, Poland's planned VAT cut from 23% to 22% was postponed due to concerns over the effects of the pandemic on public finances.

Over half of all countries have introduced temporary zero (or reduced) VAT rates for supplies of medical equipment and sanitary products (e.g. gloves, masks, hand sanitiser). Zero-rating or reduced rates have also been introduced for healthcare services where these were not yet exempt or subject to reduced rates under normal rules. The European Union introduced a six-month suspension of VAT and customs duties on the importation of medical devices and protective equipment. This measure has since been extended for another six months. Given the urgent need to accelerate vaccine deployment, the EU has also given member states the authority to diverge from the EU VAT Directive in applying a zero rate for vaccines and testing kits. Some member states have done so, and a number of non-EU countries have introduced similar measures. Several countries also implemented temporary VAT zero-rating of staff secondments to healthcare institutions and measures to safeguard the deduction of input VAT on items donated by businesses to healthcare institutions or to avoid a donation triggering any VAT liability (OECD, 2020[8]). This was the case for instance in Belgium, Chile, Colombia, Greece, Ireland, Italy, Netherlands, Poland and Thailand.

A minority of countries introduced permanent changes to their reduced VAT rates, but these were typically not related to the ongoing crisis. In particular, a number of EU countries (Austria, Greece, Lithuania and Spain) reduced VAT rates on digital publications, following an EU agreement in 2018 allowing member states to cut their VAT rates on e-publications to the reduced or zero rates applied to physical publications. Portugal permanently reduced its VAT rate on certain supplies of electricity up to a certain consumption amount to 13%.

Collection of VAT/GST on online sales by non-resident vendors and platforms

In response to increasing digitalisation and growing needs for revenue, an increasing number of countries are implementing the rules and mechanisms recommended by the OECD's International VAT/GST Guidelines to ensure the effective taxation of cross-border supplies of services and intangibles. In relation to the collection of VAT on business-to-consumer (B2C) supplies of services and intangibles made by vendors that have no physical presence in the jurisdiction of taxation, the Guidelines recommend that the right to tax these supplies for VAT purposes be allocated to the country where the consumer has its usual residence and that the foreign suppliers of these services and intangibles register and remit VAT in the country of the consumer's usual residence. The Guidelines also recommend the implementation of a simplified registration and compliance regime to facilitate tax compliance for foreign suppliers. These rules and mechanisms are particularly relevant given the continuously growing volume of online sales by offshore vendors, made directly to consumers or through the intervention of digital platforms. To date, 70 countries, including the overwhelming majority of OECD and G20 countries, have implemented or enacted rules for the application of VAT to B2C supplies of services and intangibles in line with the Guidelines. The most recent adopters of these rules and mechanisms include Chile, Indonesia, Mexico and Thailand. Many others are considering similar reforms.

The trend towards levying VAT on imports of low-value goods has also continued. A growing number of countries are removing their VAT relief regimes for imports of low-value goods in light of the rapid growth in the volume of such imports. Not levying VAT on low-value imported goods under these relief regimes is resulting in increasingly important amounts of potential VAT revenues not being collected and growing risks of unfair competition for domestic retailers that are required to charge VAT on their sales to domestic consumers. Australia was the first OECD country to implement a reform to collect GST on imports of low-value goods in 2018, in accordance with the rules and mechanisms developed by the OECD to replace the traditional collection of VAT at the border by the collection at the time of sale of the imported goods by the non-resident vendors or by the online platform. Australia was followed by New Zealand (2019), the United Kingdom (2020) and the European Union (2021). Canada will apply similar measures to non-resident vendors supplying digital products and services to consumers in Canada as of 1 July 2021 and Singapore has just announced that it will impose GST on imported low-value goods (valued up to SGD 400 and imported via air or post) that are currently not subject to GST, from 1 January 2023. All these new regimes include a liability for digital platforms such as e-commerce marketplaces to collect and remit the VAT on the imports of goods that were sold by online vendors through their platform.

Table 2.2. Temporary VAT/GST rate reductions and exemptions in OECD and G20 countries

Standard rate	General reduced rates	Restaurant meals and beverages	Tourism and hospitality	Cultural and sporting services	Specific healthcare supplies	Other[1]
Germany	China	Austria	Argentina	Argentina	Argentina[0]	Brazil[0]
Ireland	Germany	Belgium	Austria	Austria	Austria[e]	Colombia[0]
	Norway	China[0]	Belgium	Colombia[e]	Belgium[e]	Greece
		Colombia[0]	China[0]	Czech Republic	Brazil[0]	Hungary
		Germany	Colombia[0]	Greece	Canada[0]	Korea
		Hungary	Czech Republic	Netherlands	China[e]	Russia[e]
		United Kingdom	Greece	Portugal	Colombia[0]	Turkey
			Hungary	Turkey	Czech Republic[0]	Saudi Arabia
			Indonesia	United Kingdom	Finland[e]	
			Ireland		France	
			Norway		Greece[0]	
			Turkey		Ireland[0]	
			United Kingdom		Italy	
					Lithuania[0]	
					Netherlands[0]	
					Poland[0]	
					Portugal[0]	
					Russia[0]	
					Slovak Republic[0]	
					Slovenia[0]	
					Spain[0]	
					Switzerland[0]	
					United Kingdom[0]	

Note: [0] Countries that have reduced VAT/GST rates to zero for certain goods and services. [e] Countries that have introduced temporary VAT/GST exemptions. [1] Brazil introduced a temporary zero federal tax rate on listed manufacturing supplies. Colombia held a number of VAT-free days (for certain goods), declared a VAT exemption for artistic services, temporarily reduced the VAT rate for air fuel and air transport of passengers and temporarily provided a zero VAT rate for mobile phone plans. Greece allowed for a 20% reduction in the tax liability derived from reduced rents and made the VAT corresponding to hotel construction costs payable by investors. Hungary reduced the VAT rate from 27% to 5% on new dwellings for two years. Korea introduced a 70% discount on the VAT on car purchases from March 2020 to the end of June 2020. Russia introduced a zero VAT rate for software and database sales and licensing by IT companies subject to certain conditions. Saudi Arabia introduced a 5% real estate transaction tax and exempted these transactions from VAT. Turkey temporarily reduced the VAT rate from 18% to 8% for the period 31 July 2020 to 31 December 2020, which it applied to a relatively wide number of goods and services including cleaning and washing services, events and conferences, hairdressing and domestics maintenance and repairs.
Source: Country responses to the 2021 OECD Tax Policy Reforms Questionnaire, IBFD COVID-19 Tax Monitor (2021)

Excise duty changes

Excise taxes have continued to follow the trend of recent years, with a number of countries introducing taxes on a wider range of goods identified as harmful to citizens' health and an increase in the rates of existing excise taxes. (For a discussion of environmentally related excise duties, see section 2.5). The majority of countries that raised excise duties were OECD members and tax increases focused on tobacco products, tobacco substitutes and alcohol. In addition, Turkey increased excise duties on sweetened drinks, with Italy delaying the implementation of a similar tax by twelve months and Latvia announcing the introduction of an increased rate on sweetened drinks that contain a large amount of sugar in 2022. Other changes included increased excise duties on electronic products in Argentina and a higher special consumption tax rate on high-value vehicles in Turkey.

Reductions in excise taxes, waivers, and payment deferrals were less common, but nevertheless occurred in a few countries. Reductions (waivers and deferrals) in excise duties were generally limited in scope (and time) to a small number of products with specific purposes (e.g. health related goods in Brazil, alcohol for cleaning in Hungary and alcohol from specified Portuguese islands), though these changes were more general in Paraguay, where excise duties on alcohol and electronic devices were lowered.

Import and export duties

Import duties were reduced (often to a zero rate) for healthcare supplies in almost three fifths of the countries surveyed. In the majority of cases, these measures temporarily suspended customs duties on protective equipment, testing kits and medical devices such as ventilators, making it less costly to import necessary medical equipment. These measures were generally applied for an initial period of 6-12 months, though this was extended in almost all countries until at least the end of the second quarter of 2021.

A limited number of countries also altered other duties on imports and exports. For instance, Argentina introduced changes to its export duties, increasing export duties on soy products and derivatives in early 2020 before reducing these duties for three months later in the year. It also reduced export duties for several agro-industrial products, industrial and mining products and goods produced by the automotive sector in order to support foreign demand. Indonesia also provided import duty relief for air and marine transportation vehicles.

2.5. Environmentally related taxes continued to be raised in a number of countries, but were lowered in some

A number of OECD and G20 countries increased their fuel excise taxes[6] and carbon taxes, highlighting the central role of carbon pricing in climate mitigation strategies. Some countries reported reductions in their fuel excise duties, either on a temporary basis as crisis-related measures, or on a permanent basis. Some countries also increased vehicle and other transportation taxes to raise revenue and incentivise more sustainable modes of transportation, while others decreased them in response to the crisis to foster consumption and support businesses. There were few tax increases related to other tax bases, such as plastic, chemicals or waste.

Energy taxes

Six countries increased some of their fuel excise taxes (Denmark, Finland, Latvia, South Africa, Sweden, and United Kingdom). Finland and Denmark increased their energy taxes on heating fuels and South Africa increased its general fuel levy. The United Kingdom removed most reduced rates for diesel from April 2022 to better reflect the negative environmental impact of the emissions from diesel use. This will mean that most businesses across the United Kingdom that use diesel will be subject to the standard rate for diesel. Sweden abolished tax exemptions for certain renewables in heat generation and eliminated energy tax reductions for heating fuels for industry, agriculture, forestry and aquaculture. Latvia abolished its excise tax exemptions for natural gas used for heating greenhouses on agricultural land and industrial poultry holdings, and abolished its reduced excise tax rates on fuels containing bio-products.

Six countries (Denmark, Germany, Ireland, Luxembourg, the Netherlands, and South Africa) have raised explicit carbon prices, through changes to carbon taxes and emissions trading schemes. Pricing carbon emissions allows countries to smoothly steer their economies towards and along a carbon-neutral growth path. By putting a price on carbon emissions, countries can increase resource efficiency, boost investment in clean energy, develop and sell lower emission goods and services, and increase resilience to risks inherent in deep structural change. Today, however, outside the road sector, carbon emissions remain largely untaxed (OECD, 2019[10]). Even accounting for carbon prices resulting from emissions trading, most emissions are not priced at a level that reflects a low-end estimate of their climate costs (EUR 30 per tonne of CO_2) (OECD, 2018[11]).

The extent to which and how countries price carbon varies. South Africa increased its carbon tax by 5.6% for the 2020 calendar year. Accordingly, the carbon tax rate will increase by ZAR 7 (EUR 0.40) to ZAR 127 (EUR 7.25) per tonne of CO_2. Denmark also increased its taxes on greenhouse gas emissions as part of their Green Tax reform in 2020. Luxembourg introduced a CO_2 tax of EUR 31.56 per tonne of CO_2 on petrol, EUR 34.16 per tonne of CO_2 on diesel and EUR20 per tonne of CO_2 on all other energy products except electricity.[7] The tax is set to be increased to EUR 25 per tonne of CO_2 in 2022 and EUR 30 in 2023. Ireland increased its carbon tax by EUR 7.50 to EUR 33.50 per tonne of CO_2 in 2021. In the Netherlands, new carbon levies have been introduced for the power and industry sector that set a minimum price on carbon emissions from facilities that are covered by the EU ETS (Anderson et al., 2021[12]). In industry, a key feature of the levy is the combination of a pre-defined price trajectory with a levy base that phases in over time. The levy starts at EUR 30 per tonne of CO_2 in 2021 and reaches EUR 125 per tonne in 2030. Germany introduced a national emissions trading system (nETS), covering carbon emissions of upstream energy suppliers for transport and heating purposes in non-EU ETS sectors. In 2021, emissions allowances are being sold at a fixed price of EUR 25 per tonne of CO_2 and are set to be sold for EUR 55 per tonne in 2025. Starting 2026, the price will be determined by auctions within a pre-defined price corridor of EUR 55-65 per tonne of CO_2. ETSs and carbon taxes can be equally effective and efficient, depending on the details of their design.

On the other hand, some countries reduced some of their fuel excise duties (the Czech Republic, Estonia, Latvia, Sweden, and the United Kingdom). In Latvia and the United Kingdom, the measures are temporary. Latvia temporarily reduced its tax rate on natural gas used as propellant, and the United Kingdom froze its fuel tax rates for 2020-21. The Czech Republic and Estonia reduced their excise duty on diesel. Estonia also reduced its excise duties for gasoline, natural gas, and electricity (in part as a response to the COVID-19 crisis, but also to decrease cross-border refuelling in Latvia and Lithuania). Sweden introduced an exemption for bio propane as a heating fuel, and Italy abolished its regional tax on petrol for motor vehicles.

Denmark and Finland reduced their taxes on electricity to encourage electrification, in line with OECD recommendations (OECD, 2019[10]). Finland decreased its tax on electricity for industry, agriculture and data centres to the European minimum, which was accompanied by gradual abolition of the energy tax refunds for energy-intensive enterprises. Denmark decreased its taxes on electricity and postponed a temporary energy tax. Sweden, on the other hand, introduced higher taxes on certain uses of electricity.

Vehicle and other transport taxes

A few countries and jurisdictions introduced mostly temporary decreases in their road or motor vehicle taxes. Temporary measures were introduced by the Czech Republic, Japan, and Macau. The Czech Republic temporarily reduced its road tax on trucks by 25%, Japan temporarily reduced its environmental performance excise tax on cars, and Macau waived its annual motor vehicle tax for 2020. Permanent measures included Slovenia's motor vehicle tax reform, which is determined by CO_2 emissions and fuel consumption and resulted in a decrease of the tax.

Other countries raised their vehicle taxes. Japan reclassified its excise tax rate on the environmental performance of cars in line with 2030 fuel efficiency standards. As a result, certain diesel vehicles previously considered as 'clean' are no longer excluded from the excise tax. Denmark also reformed its motor vehicle taxes to further promote environmental standards. Germany reformed its motor vehicle tax by increasing the climate component (CO_2 emissions[8]) alongside cubic capacity to the motor vehicle tax as of 1 January 2021. The Netherlands implemented stricter CO_2 requirements and increased its motor vehicle tax, with the requirements legislated in 2020 and entering into force in 2021. Latvia introduced a new company car tax rate for vehicles with large engine capacity, and indexed its company car tax rates to inflation. The Seychelles increased their excise tax rate on vehicles by 25%.

There were a few changes to air travel taxes. Germany marginally reduced its air travel tax rates in 2021 and Norway temporarily abolished its air passenger and aviation tax for 2020. Austria, the Netherlands, and Portugal, on the other hand, increased or introduced air travel taxes. Austria increased its flight ticket tax to, in particular, deter short-haul flights. Before the reform, short-haul, medium-haul, and long-haul flights were taxed at EUR 3.50, EUR 7.50, and EUR 17.50 per ticket respectively. Since September 2020, the standard flight ticket tax is EUR 12 and for very short flights under 350 kilometres, the tax is EUR 30 per ticket. The Netherlands introduced an air passenger tax of EUR 7.45 per passenger applying to all passengers departing from a Dutch airport from 1 January 2021. Portugal introduced a EUR 2 fee per passenger for air and sea travel.

Other environmentally related taxes

Environmentally related tax reforms related to other tax bases (e.g. plastic, chemicals or waste) continued to be rare, with a few countries introducing or increasing taxes in this area (e.g. Latvia, Sweden, and the United Kingdom). Latvia increased its natural resource tax rates on waste disposal and pollution Sweden introduced a tax on hazardous chemicals in clothing and footwear. The United Kingdom will introduce a Plastic Packaging Tax from 2022, with a rate of GBR 200 per tonne of plastic packaging containing less than 30% recycled materials. The tax had been announced in 2018 and is intended to provide a clear economic incentive for businesses to use recycled material in the production of plastic packaging, which may create greater demand for this material in the future.

2.6. Property taxes were reduced in some countries to address liquidity concerns, while others increased them to meet growing revenue needs

Relatively few governments introduced changes to property taxes over the last year, but those that did generally sought to ease costs for struggling businesses and households. Liquidity support to businesses was provided through measures including business property tax deferrals and waivers, which were often targeted at severely affected businesses. A few countries also reduced their property transaction taxes, often to support housing markets. On the other hand, some countries increased their property taxes, particularly those targeting high-wealth taxpayers as a way to meet their growing revenue needs and enhance equity.

Business property taxes

The payment of business property taxes has been deferred or waived in a number of countries, mainly to relieve operating cost pressures for those sectors hit hardest by the pandemic (e.g. Bulgaria, Chile, Israel, Italy, Japan, Peru, Singapore and the United Kingdom). In Italy, Singapore and the United Kingdom, recurrent taxes on immovable property (and/or land-use fees) were waived for businesses that suffered the most significant restrictions on activity, such as those operating in the hospitality, retail, and leisure sectors. In Israel, businesses that registered a significant fall in revenues during the first six months of the pandemic were provided with a substantial reduction in recurrent municipal taxes on immovable property until June 2021. A similar measure was introduced in Japan, whereby SMEs could receive a 50% discount or full reduction in the fixed assets tax and city planning tax on depreciable assets and business buildings for the fiscal year 2021, depending on the extent of the fall in business income experienced. At the onset of the pandemic, Bulgaria also extended the deadline for payment of its real estate taxes (for both business and homeowners) by two months and provided a 5% discount on the total tax due. In Peru, an exceptional expedited refund of the temporary tax on net assets was provided to those businesses who filed corporate income tax returns. Chile introduced measures to enable SMEs to defer instalments of property tax payments during 2020.

Very few business property tax rate reductions were reported. In Macau, there were two separate temporary cuts in the commercial property tax for 2020, while the Canadian provinces of British Columbia and Ontario both permanently reduced business education taxes for commercial properties.

Recurrent taxes on residential property

Residential property owners also benefitted from tax waivers and payment deferrals in some countries. All residential property was exempted from taxation for 2020 in Macau, while in Greece measures to reduce the real estate tax (ENFIA) and provide exemptions to its supplementary component, which were implemented for 2019, were extended for 2020. In Chile, measures to enable low- and middle-income homeowners to defer instalments of property tax payments were extended during 2020. The Seychelles also extended the tax registration, submission and payment periods for the new property tax owed by non-Seychellois unable to travel to the island during the pandemic.

On the other hand, Korea introduced comprehensive real estate tax reforms with the objectives of raising additional revenue, stabilising the housing market and enhancing fairness. The reform to the recurrent property tax regime introduces new tax rates that increase with three factors: firstly, the number of properties owned by the taxpayer; secondly, where multiple property owners register themselves as rental business operators; and thirdly, where land is more valuable.

Property transaction taxes

A number of OECD countries reduced their property transaction taxes. Temporary cuts were introduced in the United Kingdom, where the starting threshold value at which properties are subject to transaction taxes in England and Northern Ireland was increased by a factor of four – this temporary measure was extended by a further three months from its original end date. Other countries introduced permanent property transaction tax reductions. Real estate transaction taxes were abolished completely in the Czech Republic. In Israel, a decrease in the tax rate on immovable property transactions was introduced six months earlier than originally announced. The Netherlands introduced a number of changes to its property transaction tax, including a new exemption for first time home buyers under the age of 35 to enhance housing affordability. On the other hand, there was an increase in the Dutch transaction tax rate on non-residential real estate from 7% to 8%. In Korea the securities transaction tax was reduced by 0.02 percentage points in 2021, with a further 0.08 percentage points reduction announced for 2023.

Net wealth taxes

A few countries increased or introduced new taxes on net wealth in order to meet their growing needs for tax revenue, some of which have been temporary and others permanent. Argentina introduced a one-off tax on the net wealth of residents that own assets worth more than ARS 200 million (around EUR 1.85 million), while Spain increased its net wealth tax rate from 2.5% to 3.5% in the top wealth tax bracket (worldwide assets exceeding approximately EUR 10.7 million). Belgium introduced a 0.15% recurrent tax on the holding of a securities account, which is levied on the average value of the account in excess of EUR 1 million during the reference period, with the first reference period being 27 February 2021 to 30 September 2021. Prior to the COVID-19 crisis, Colombia established a temporary tax on the net wealth of individuals who are considered income taxpayers and non-resident individuals as well as certain foreign companies for 2020-2021, who declared domestic equity holdings of above EUR 1.18 million in the previous two years. On the other hand, Norway reduced taxpayers' liabilities under the net wealth tax by permanently increasing the valuation discount for shares and operating assets from 25% initially to 35% and subsequently to 45%, while company owners with expected losses for 2020 were allowed to defer the payment of net wealth taxes.

References

Anderson, B. et al. (2021), "Policies for a climate-neutral industry: Lessons from the Netherlands", *OECD Science, Technology and Industry Policy Papers*, No. 108, OECD Publishing, Paris, https://dx.doi.org/10.1787/a3a1f953-en. [12]

Banque de France (2021), *Business failures: February 2021*, https://www.banque-france.fr/en/statistics/key-figures-france-and-abroad/business-failures. [4]

Deutsche Bundesbank (2020), *Monthly Report, November 2020: The German Economy*, https://www.bundesbank.de/en/publications/reports/monthly-reports/current-monthly-reports--764440. [6]

Giacomelli, S., S. Mocetti and G. Rodano (2021), "Fallimenti D'Impresa in Epoca COVID", *Banca d'Italia Note Covid-19*, https://www.bancaditalia.it/pubblicazioni/note-covid-19/2021/2021.0.1.27-ciclo.economico.fallimenti-nota.covid.pdf. [5]

IMF (2021), *Fiscal Monitor Update, January 2021*, IMF Publishing, Washington, DC, https://www.imf.org/en/Publications/FM/Issues/2021/01/20/fiscal-monitor-update-january-2021. [1]

OECD (2021), "Supporting jobs and companies: A bridge to the recovery phase", *OECD Policy Responses to Coronavirus (COVID-19)*, pp. Paris, OECD Publishing, https://doi.org/10.1787/08962553-en. [3]

OECD (2020), *Consumption Tax Trends 2020: VAT/GST and Excise Rates, Trends and Policy Issues*, OECD Publishing, Paris, https://dx.doi.org/10.1787/152def2d-en. [8]

OECD (2020), *Coronavirus (COVID-19): SME policy responses*, OECD Publishing, Paris, https://doi.org/10.1787/04440101-en. [9]

OECD (2020), *Corporate Tax Statisticss: Second Edition*, OECD Publishing, Paris, http://www.oecd.org/tax/tax-policy/corporate-tax-statistics-second-edition.pdf. [7]

OECD (2020), "Special Feature: Tax and fiscal policy responses to the COVID-19 crisis", in *Tax Policy Reforms 2020: OECD and Selected Partner Economies*, OECD Publishing, Paris, https://dx.doi.org/10.1787/da2badac-en. [2]

OECD (2019), *Taxing Energy Use 2019: Using Taxes for Climate Action*, OECD Publishing, Paris, https://dx.doi.org/10.1787/058ca239-en. [10]

OECD (2018), *Effective Carbon Rates 2018: Pricing Carbon Emissions Through Taxes and Emissions Trading*, OECD Publishing, Paris, https://dx.doi.org/10.1787/9789264305304-en. [11]

Notes

[1] The measure concerns employees with personal taxable income over EUR 28 000, starting from an amount of EUR 1 200 and decreasing gradually to EUR 960 at personal taxable income of EUR 35 000. Above EUR 35 000, the tax credit decreases gradually to EUR 0 at taxable income of EUR 40 000.

[2] Originally, when the measure was introduced in June 2020, it was designed to temporarily apply to tax years 2020 and 2021. In December 2020, however, Germany decided to make the increase in the single-parent income tax allowance permanent.

[3] Eligible educators include any individual who is a kindergarten through grade 12 teacher, instructor, counsellor, principal, or aide in a school for at least 900 hours during a school year.

[4] The tax credits can be transferred to hotels, construction companies as well as financial intermediaries.

[5] South Africa has three different standard deductions that apply to different age groups.

[6] Unlike explicit carbon taxes and carbon prices resulting from emissions trading systems, fuel excise taxes are usually not levied with environmental or climate reasons in mind, but are administratively and economically similar to carbon taxes and are hence classified as carbon pricing instruments in OECD work (OECD, 2019[10]).

[7] Sectors falling under the EU-ETS system are exempt from the CO_2 tax.

[8] The tax is set to increase in six levels from EUR 2 to EUR 4 for each gram over 95 grams of carbon dioxide emitted per kilometre.

3 Way forward

This Chapter offers some guidance as to how tax policy responses could be adapted in the future. It identifies guiding principles on how countries can improve the targeting of emergency relief and carefully withdraw it as they emerge from the grip of the pandemic and loosen mobility and other restrictions. It also provides some guidance on how to design and implement effective stimulus-oriented tax measures. It concludes by providing a brief overview of the work that the OECD will be undertaking to help countries reassess their tax and spending policies in the longer run.

Today, the priority for countries is to continue adapting their fiscal response to the evolving health and economic developments. Governments should continue to use fiscal tools to provide relief to severely affected businesses and households where recovery remains hampered by containment measures, mobility restrictions or slow vaccinations. As economies reopen and economic activity rebounds, where possible, fiscal policy should remain supportive of the recovery.

Once the recovery is firmly in place, countries should re-examine their tax and spending policies to ensure that they address the structural economic challenges they face. These assessments will need to account for both the difficulties accentuated by the crisis, including increased debt levels, as well as those related to ongoing structural challenges including climate change, population ageing, rising inequalities, and digitalisation. This assessment process will then enable countries to determine the combination of fiscal policies needed to deliver inclusive, resilient and sustainable economic growth as they move beyond the pandemic.

Governments' responses to the ongoing crisis will naturally be tailored to country-specific circumstances, but there are some general guiding principles that countries can follow. The severity of the crisis, risks of longer-term scarring effects and countries' fiscal positions will all be determining factors in governments' responses to the pandemic and its aftermath. Nevertheless, this chapter offers some broad guiding principles to address two significant tax policy challenges faced by almost all countries in the short run, namely the withdrawal of relief where it is no longer needed and the provision of well-designed recovery-oriented stimulus measures. It also gives a brief overview of the work that the OECD will be undertaking in the future to help countries reassess their tax and spending priorities and policies in the longer run.

3.1. In the short run, a careful approach to tax relief and stimulus is needed

Emergency tax relief: increased targeting and careful withdrawal

Government approaches to tax relief will require a delicate balancing act. It will require ensuring that businesses and households severely affected by the crisis continue to receive sufficient support, while limiting the pressure on public budgets and ensuring a sustainable recovery by removing relief where it is no longer needed. However, the blunt and poorly timed withdrawal of relief could pose serious risks. As fiscal support is withdrawn and deferred tax payments come due, corporate cash flow might be put under severe pressure, creating a drag on economic recovery and possibly leading to an increase in corporate financial distress and business failures. Thus, relief withdrawal should be undertaken carefully.

Avoiding the premature withdrawal of relief and extending cash flow and income support measures where needed

The costs of removing support too early are likely to be greater than the costs of removing support later. Given the protracted nature of the crisis, with containment measures still significantly constraining supply and demand in many countries and the high level of uncertainty, governments should avoid prematurely withdrawing support. Support should be maintained where it is needed to keep businesses and households afloat. Withdrawing support too soon to businesses and households in need poses serious risks, including mass bankruptcies and job losses. Countries need to take heed of their experiences from the 2007-2009 crisis. After the financial crisis, policymakers were "flying blind" in that they had little research to guide them at that time, which had an impact on the way they designed and later withdrew stimulus packages (Ramey, 2019[1]). Overall, evidence shows that stimulus was withdrawn too early, which resulted in a prolonged period of slow sub-par growth. Nevertheless, every crisis is different and the speed of improvements in the health situation and the relaxation of containment measures will be the key determinant of whether, and the pace at which, emergency relief measures can be reduced and ultimately withdrawn.

Some measures play an important role in supporting liquidity and cash flow and are less costly to extend than others. For instance, tax payment deferrals and waivers of late payment interest and fines might be important for businesses and households still facing hardship, but may not be all that costly in terms of tax revenue foregone (as long as businesses survive the crisis). These measures could be extended, although in a more targeted way, until economic activity returns to normal. Loss carry-back measures could also be introduced or extended to enhance cash flow and target lossmaking firms (which were previously profitable) that will typically not benefit from other tax measures such as rate reductions or exemptions. While these measures involve an immediate revenue cost for governments, it is likely to be relatively low as it merely changes the timing of when losses are used to offset taxable income. This is particularly the case if these provisions are used by businesses that will be viable after the crisis. Additional tax measures that countries could consider introducing or extending to provide relief to businesses include accelerated tax refunds, revisions to income tax prepayment calculations to reflect anticipated drops in revenue, or recurrent business property tax waivers for struggling businesses. Increasing the limits to the deductibility of interest payments from taxable business income could also be considered on a temporary basis but should avoid creating opportunities for tax planning and windfall gains.

Governments should also prioritise removing tax hurdles to the production and deployment of vital equipment and vaccines. Rolling out the vaccine strategy remains the key priority both from a health and economic perspective. The tax system should not create any hurdles for the production or importation of vaccines. The European Union, for instance, has given EU Member States the authority to diverge from the EU VAT Directive in applying a zero VAT rate for vaccines and testing kits (European Commission, 2020[2]). Countries should ensure that their VAT and customs duty rules are adjusted and that they communicate the new rules to the business sector so that the importation of vital equipment and vaccines can be facilitated in an orderly and swift manner.

Progressively replacing blanket measures with more targeted support

Targeted tax relief can help strike a balance between ensuring that support is delivered to those who need it most, while limiting the fiscal cost of such measures. Increased targeting also implies that the amount of support that can be provided to those in need can be larger. This is particularly necessary given the highly uneven impact of the crisis across different sectors, businesses and households and the forecast that the recovery is likely to be highly uneven too (see Chapter 1).

Countries have increasingly moved away from broad-based containment measures to more targeted ones, and more information has become available on the economic and distributional impacts of the crisis as it has progressed. At the start of the crisis, when support was critically needed across the economy given broad-based lockdowns and when relatively little information was available on the types of businesses and households that were most affected, targeting would have almost certainly resulted in an under-provision of support and less timely relief. However, as the crisis has unfolded and countries have increasingly moved away from broad-based lockdowns, governments have more accurate information regarding the sectors, types of businesses, households or regions that may require continued emergency relief.

Relief should increasingly be targeted at taxpayers who need it the most. Support should be targeted at the most vulnerable households. The crisis has exacerbated existing inequalities (OECD, 2020[3]). In particular, those sectors affected by confinement measures, comprising large shares of low-skilled workers, have suffered extreme income losses, while labour markets for many higher-income workers have hardly deteriorated at all (OECD, 2020[4]; Palomino, Rodriguez and Sebastian, 2020[5]). Continued emergency relief should also be targeted to businesses that remain severely affected by containment measures and other constraints, such as travel restrictions. It can be targeted at particular types of businesses such as SMEs or economic sectors, or at companies that have experienced a significant and persistent drop in revenue relative to pre-crisis years. In sectors that are still subject to significant restrictions, access to relief measures should remain automatic for most companies, while in sectors that have been able to resume activities, relief could be granted on a more selective or even case-by-case basis, following a specific request from businesses, with reference to additional eligibility requirements. These eligibility requirements should be clearly and transparently communicated to businesses so they can verify whether and how they can apply.

Targeting prolonged relief only at firms that are likely to be viable post-pandemic may be desirable, but difficult to implement in practice. In many cases, measures aimed at providing relief to viable firms have also allowed unviable firms to survive. Support to unviable firms implies that part of the relief could have been better allocated to more productive businesses with a better prognosis of future success, which could ultimately slow the recovery, and potentially result in significant tax revenue losses for governments if businesses that have received tax support go bankrupt. However, this crisis makes it particularly difficult to distinguish viable from non-viable firms. For instance, a July 2020 study in France showed that highly productive firms accounted for a disproportionate share of companies facing insolvency (Guerini et al., 2020[6]). Care should be taken not to withdraw support prematurely for firms that are viable yet facing liquidity constraints, which could jeopardise their existence. More generally, applying traditional criteria to identify "viable" businesses – such as balance sheet data or recent credit history – may be more difficult given the scale and uniqueness of the shock countries have experienced (OECD, 2020[7]). Assessing firm viability is also particularly challenging where sectors remain severely constrained by containment measures. A further element of uncertainty hampering efforts to assess firm viability is the fact that the current pandemic has evinced a whole range of dramatic shifts in consumption and production behaviours and the permanence of some of these changes will only be known over time. However, targeting firms based on assessment of future viability may become easier over time and as sectors resume their activities under near (or 'new') normal conditions.

Avoiding "cliff edge" effects

The removal of short-term relief measures should avoid sudden spikes in tax liabilities. The removal of measures such as tax deferrals should not generate sudden increases in tax liabilities, or "cliff edge" effects that could result in solvency problems for recovering businesses. This can be achieved by progressively phasing out relief measures or by replacing initial relief measures with new ones.

More generally, extending cash flow support measures should avoid storing up problems for the future, making it more difficult for taxpayers to return to normal if, for example, debts build up to unsustainable levels or deferred payments lead to severe cash flow problems at a later date. For instance, the longer tax deferrals are extended, the higher the risks that deferred tax payments reach unsustainable levels later. Such problems could be minimised by turning tax payment deferrals into interest-free tax payment plans (e.g. fixed monthly or quarterly payments of the tax due spread over several months or years). Tax payment plans could possibly be made sector or firm-specific to tailor them to the specific challenges faced by sectors or individual businesses. Additional difficulties may arise where governments have provided loan guarantees allowing firms to take out additional loans to survive the crisis. The additional debt taken on by businesses will increase interest payments that are due, which could increase solvency risks in particular if the economic recovery is slow. Governments may therefore have to extend support into the recovery phase to ensure that viable firms survive the crisis once the pandemic is under control.

Carefully enforcing and monitoring relief measures

Careful enforcement of relief measures and preventing potential abuse is critical. For instance, measures to accelerate refunds of VAT credits and other taxes, and payment of direct financial support more generally, can be vulnerable to abuse during times of crisis as cash-strapped businesses may be tempted to file fraudulent claims. This may be particularly true for countries with weaker tax auditing tools and capabilities. Where this is the case, tax administrations may consider restricting the availability of certain measures, such as the accelerated payment of VAT refunds, to businesses with a good compliance record or capping the amounts of accelerated refunds. This could be complemented with temporary measures to focus tax administration capacity on issues specific to the crisis, such as assessing and monitoring taxpayers and tax issues that present particular compliance risks as a result of the crisis through basic compliance indicators such as late filings and the evolution of tax arrears, and proactively contacting selected taxpayers to provide targeted assistance. Cases of abuse should also be sanctioned through clearly communicated fines and clawback measures.

Monitoring and regular data analysis is also essential to ensure that measures achieve their objectives. Regular monitoring and data collection are critical to determining whether fiscal provisions should be extended, reduced, removed or recalibrated to ensure that relief reaches the right sectors, firms and households. Monitoring and data analysis are also key to ensuring that tax relief does not lead to unintended effects (e.g. property tax waiver in the United Kingdom driving an increase in housing prices). The availability of high-frequency data (e.g. from credit cards) and forecasts based on quasi real-time data may help governments to determine the best policy strategies and actions.

Care should be taken around engagement with taxpayers, clear communication and providing some degree of stability. Anecdotal evidence suggests that in many countries there has been a strong positive reaction by taxpayers to the actions taken by tax administrations in helping to address cash flow concerns and reducing burdens on taxpayers, as well as to the role played by some tax administrations in the provision of government support. As is the case for fiscal support, care should be taken to avoid a "cliff edge" in terms of changes in messaging or a return to pre-crisis compliance activities by tax administrations where they have been suspended or reduced. Consideration should be given as to how to best communicate the rationale and timing of resumption of more normal operations to avoid adversely impacting taxpayer attitudes which might in turn adversely affect compliance behaviours. Providing a reasonable level of stability is also key. The proliferation of short-term measures and frequent changes to existing measures should be carefully assessed to avoid creating additional complexities for taxpayers.

Pursuing well-designed stimulus

As economies reopen, recovery-oriented stimulus measures could play a significant role if demand and investment remain persistently low. Stimulus policies should be considered if, once the pandemic is under control and activities are largely allowed to resume, consumption and investment remain persistently low.

Evidence suggests that fiscal stimulus may be particularly effective in the current context. Fiscal multipliers tend to be higher when monetary policy is very accommodative and interest rates remain low (Christiano, Eichenbaum and Rebelo, 2011[8]; Woodford, 2011[9]; Coenen et al., 2012[10]; Erceg and Lindé, 2014[11]) as is currently the case (see Chapter 1). In addition, fiscal policy has the advantage of being deployed through a variety of tools and channels, which allows it to have more direct and selective effects than monetary policy (Bartsch, Bénassy-Quéré and Corset, 2020[12]).

Nevertheless, fiscal stimulus should be carefully designed and adapted to country circumstances to ensure that it is effective. In particular, stimulus should be carefully timed and introduced when the health situation improves and economies reopen. The size of the stimulus package is also going to depend on the speed at which economies rebound: larger and more prolonged stimulus measures might be needed where recovery is anaemic, but where economies rebound strongly, the size and length of stimulus packages can be curtailed. Under certain circumstances, large stimulus packages could also increase risks of rising inflation, especially as there will likely be pent-up demand in many countries, which was one of the reasons why the rebound in the second half of 2020 was so strong (see Chapter 1). While rising inflation could lead to an increase in interest rates and affect debt sustainability, some inflation may be welcome in the current context. Stimulus measures should also be aligned with countries' longer term environmental, health and social challenges. More generally, policy flexibility will be key: this crisis is making conventional stimulus policies somewhat less effective under continued restrictions and the adequate timing of policies more difficult, so flexibly adapting policies to changing health and economic circumstances will be critical.

Getting the timing right

The introduction of recovery-oriented stimulus measures should be timely. In particular, introducing stimulus measures while lockdowns or severe restrictions are still in place will largely be ineffective and can even go against the objective of containing the spread of the virus. There is evidence that some of the tax stimulus measures introduced after the first wave of the pandemic have had less of an impact than anticipated because they were introduced when restrictions were still in place (OECD, 2021[13]). An additional challenge is potential time lags between the design of policies, their enactment, their implementation, take-up by taxpayers and the receipt of benefits by taxpayers.

In many cases, relief and stimulus measures are likely to coexist. This combination of measures is unusual when compared to previous economic crises, but will be necessary given the unique nature of the ongoing crisis. Many countries have introduced partial lockdowns, allowing some businesses to resume activities, while others, such as tourism and hospitality, remain severely constrained. Many countries have also adopted intermittent approaches where containment measures are relaxed and then tightened again as renewed outbreak risks arise. This has increased heterogeneous effects across businesses and households, which should be taken into consideration in countries' policy responses. The mix of relief and recovery-oriented stimulus measures should therefore be closely aligned with the nature of the containment and mitigation measures in place. For instance, where containment measures are partially lifted, businesses that are still subject to restrictions may need continued liquidity and solvency support, while sectors that can resume their activities could benefit from stimulus measures.

Ensuring that stimulus is temporary

Recovery-oriented tax measures should be temporary. Temporary stimulus encourages businesses and households to bring their spending and investments forward. Without an end date to the measures, there is less incentive to do so. There is also evidence that the timing of investment decisions tends to react strongly to taxation (US Treasury, 2010[14]). In addition, temporary stimulus has the advantage of limiting the impact of measures on public budgets. Stimulus measures could also have pro-cyclical effects if they are maintained once economic recovery is on a solid footing.

Measures could have clear end dates but allow for possible temporary extensions, or be tied to the achievement of certain outcomes. Measures could have clearly specified expiry dates or sunset clauses. This would induce government to evaluate the effectiveness of measures. However, given the uncertainty of the pandemic, some flexibility may be needed. If there is a strong case for extending measures once their expiry date is reached to continue supporting supply or demand, these could be temporarily extended. For instance, debt overhangs built up by businesses, households or the financial sector may lead to longer than anticipated weakness in consumption and investment while debts are being paid down. In these cases, the temporary extension of measures beyond their initially anticipated end-dates may be warranted. An alternative to sunset clauses may be to link the duration of stimulus measures to the attainment of certain outcomes. For instance, unemployment benefits could be maintained if unemployment rates exceed a certain threshold (Schnabel, 2021[15]; OECD, 2021[13]). Tying the duration of stimulus measures to the attainment of certain outcomes (e.g. recovery in certain sectors, employment levels) may reduce risks of discontinued or delayed support where discretionary extensions may need to be approved through long legislative processes.

Targeting stimulus to areas where equity needs and fiscal multipliers are highest

Targeting support at less affluent households, in addition to being fairer, is likely to have a greater impact on output. As mentioned above, the crisis has had a highly uneven impact across households and the recovery is expected to be unequal too. Therefore, targeting income support at lower income households is key from an inclusiveness perspective. Targeted income support to lower income households is also expected to have higher multiplier effects as research suggests that lower income households are more likely to spend as opposed to save additional disposable income received through fiscal stimulus packages relative to other households (Sahm, Shapiro and Slemrod, 2010[16]; Parker et al., 2013[17]; Broda and Parker, 2014[18]). A limiting factor, however, may be that households may use some portion of support as precautionary savings, or to repay debt, if they face prolonged uncertainty over unemployment prospects, dampening the multiplier effect on output (Mody, Ohnsorge and Sandri, 2012[19]; Baiardi, Magnani and Menegatti, 2019[20]; BNP Paribas, 2021[21]). This highlights the importance of ensuring that income support goes hand-in-hand with employment support measures and other measures aimed at enhancing consumer and business confidence (see Chapter 1).

Countries can provide income support to low-income households in various ways, including through cash transfers, expanded access to social benefits as well as targeted tax measures. Enhanced cash transfers or social benefits can provide cash more quickly to the ones in need, but targeted tax measures can mimic that effect for instance through advanced payments of refundable child or other types of tax credits. The effectiveness of PIT reductions in delivering support to low-income households, as well as their multiplier effects, will depend on whether significant shares of low-income households are subject to the PIT. Where most low-income households are not subject to the PIT, as is the case in many developing and emerging economies, and in some OECD countries, enhanced transfers and access to social benefits will generally be more effective in delivering support to low-income households.

On the other hand, measures to stimulate consumption, particularly broad-based and untargeted ones, might not generate much additional consumption and should be carefully considered depending on country context. Many households, and particularly those with higher-incomes who have accumulated more savings during the pandemic, will be eager to consume once restrictions are lifted. This does not apply to all households as those at the lower end of the income spectrum have often experienced an increase in spending on essential consumption during lockdowns. Providing targeted income support to lower income households would therefore be more cost-effective than broad-based measures to stimulate consumption, such as VAT rate reductions, which are very costly, might not be needed to boost consumption, and would end up partly subsidising the consumption of high-income households. Targeted income support may be more difficult, however, in countries with less well developed tax and transfer systems. Tax measures favouring consumption may also have unintended consequences, such as contributing to a large increase in demand, which could drive prices up. Therefore, measures aimed at boosting consumption should be carefully considered and designed in ways that avoid providing windfall gains to higher income households.

In the area of corporate taxation, expenditure-based corporate tax incentives lead to greater additionality, in terms of new investment and job creation, than profit-based ones. Expenditure-based tax incentives, including for instance investment tax credits, accelerated depreciation allowances or immediate expensing may be effective stimulus measures, in particular if they are time-bound. They reduce the cost of capital and encourage frontloading private investment (Edge and Rudd, 2011[22]; Zwick and Mahon, 2017[23]). Such incentives should be preferred to profit-based tax incentives, which typically lead to little additionality and generate windfall gains. For instance, corporate income tax holidays can disproportionately benefit larger and more profitable firms whose investment plans would likely occur irrespective of tax holidays. Expenditure-based tax incentives also have a more immediate effect as corporations can benefit from such incentives as soon as they make an investment.

Governments could consider more generous expenditure-based tax incentives targeted at severely affected sectors. The impact of the crisis has hit a number of services sectors particularly hard, and tax support to return to normal business activities might be very welcome once the health crisis is under control and the economy recovers. In addition, expenditure-based tax incentives should be accompanied by adequate loss carry-forward provisions to ensure that tax incentives also benefit investments with delayed returns.

Prioritising measures that support employment

The crisis has led to unprecedented job losses and could have longer term scarring effects on labour markets. While labour market conditions are improving slowly, across the OECD economies, almost 10 million more people are unemployed than prior to the crisis, inactivity rates have risen and employment rates have declined (see Chapter 1). In addition, unemployment levels may rise in a number of countries when government support is withdrawn, particularly where unviable businesses are currently being propped up. In developing countries, substantial job losses have increased poverty and deprivation of millions of workers. The COVID-19 crisis is also having a greater impact on some workers than others. Young people and women are among those at greatest risk of joblessness and poverty. They generally have less secure, lower-skilled jobs and are overrepresented among workers in industries most affected by the crisis, such as tourism and restaurants. Supporting labour market recovery is therefore not only essential to ensure an economic rebound, but also to prevent intergenerational, socio-economic and gender inequalities from being further exacerbated.

Tax measures can be used to encourage businesses to retain their workers and hire new employees. Temporary and targeted reductions in employer social security contributions, either through lower contribution rates or tax credits that can be claimed against employer SSCs, may be among the measures that countries could consider. Such measures were implemented in the aftermath of the 2008/9 crisis in many countries. In addition to creating an incentive for employers to hire new workers, they reduce the cost of employing current workers, which would support business cash flow. Depending on country-specific circumstances, countries may prefer to target measures at specific categories of employers or workers (e.g. low-income or younger workers). Countries may also consider adapting support measures over time. For instance, tax support could initially be widely available to all low-income workers and then gradually recalibrated to target workers employed on indefinite contracts and/or to target specific sectors if recovery proves slower in certain sectors.

Tax measures could also be used to encourage workers to return to the labour market and, where appropriate, support re-skilling. The crisis will very likely have long-lasting effects and may have increased the speed of the structural economic changes that were set to happen as a result of, for instance, the digitalisation of the economy. Workers that have lost their jobs in less viable economic sectors or firms might be encouraged to find jobs in other sectors through, for instance, enhanced earned income tax credits. Targeted tax support for workers to re-skill might also be considered, in addition to standard active labour market policies and improved access to flexible, modular training for lower-skilled workers. It should be mentioned as well that in some cases there may be trade-offs between measures supporting productivity-enhancing investments and support for employment, especially in the short run.

Considering measures to encourage business recapitalisation

The capital structure and solvency of companies have been severely affected by the current crisis. Many firms have survived the crisis by tapping into their available cash reserves and capital stock and by taking on additional debt, weakening their capital structure and jeopardising their survival. Low levels of retained earnings could also put a drag on investment in the coming years. Policy responses have largely focused on providing liquidity support, and these policies might put the solvency of businesses under pressure if they are abruptly withdrawn. Evidence shows that in some cases support to address liquidity shortages has increased concerns over future solvency risks (IMF, 2020[24]; OECD, 2020[7]). Moreover, many firms entered the crisis with a high degree of leverage. Governments may therefore have to start turning their attention to measures that can mitigate these insolvency risks for businesses that are otherwise viable. Solvency risks might be particularly high for SMEs, which have been hit harder by the crisis than large companies (see Chapter 1) and have fewer financing options.

In light of these financing challenges, governments could consider tax measures to encourage business recapitalisation. Measures could include allowing companies to exempt part of their profits by recording them under a capital reserve aimed at rebuilding their equity. Such schemes would have to be temporary and could be capped or targeted at SMEs. Strict rules would also be needed to prevent any abuse. Temporary tax measures taken exceptionally during this period to support business recapitalisation would need to be coordinated with other policy tools, including for instance efforts to privilege grants, and equity-type support over debt for SMEs.

Aligning stimulus with longer term environmental, health and social objectives

Supporting innovation efforts through targeted support for promising clean technologies can encourage recovery and help accelerate the transition to a carbon-neutral economy. The need for low-carbon innovation and the potential for spill-overs justify targeted support for R&D and technology transfer towards specific applications, including through corporate tax incentives. If well designed, they can encourage investment in specific technologies (Maffini, Xing and Devereux, 2019[25]). Targeted technology support that generates low-carbon investment can reduce the cost of complying with carbon pricing in the future, and can become a powerful tool in building support for stronger carbon pricing. Targeted low-carbon innovation support has increasingly become a practicable option given international advances in the classification of clean technologies and standards. Where such standards for clean products and processes exist, they could be used to direct targeted support.

Such tools are even more effective when combined with carbon pricing efforts. Carbon pricing reinforces green stimulus measures and helps align traditional stimulus with climate objectives, even when it is not explicitly targeted towards decarbonisation. Carbon taxes or emissions trading systems encourage cleaner investment and consumption choices for all public and private spending, limiting CO_2 emissions and local pollution. Tax and spending policies can be implemented in tandem to deliver an equitable reform package that boosts the purchasing power of vulnerable groups (OECD, 2020[26]).

Where raising carbon prices is not an immediate policy option, governments could usefully commit to future price increases (Van Dender and Teusch, 2020[27]). Expectations about higher future carbon prices can create strong incentives, particularly for investments in long-lived assets and infrastructure. Households and businesses will embrace low carbon on their own if they believe that carbon prices will rise over time, without the need for the government to identify the most promising technologies and spending choices in advance. This reduces the risk of stranded assets and stranded jobs in the future.

Investment incentives could also be used to steer businesses towards investments that minimise health-related risks or strengthen the collective ability to respond to such risks in the future. For instance, special tax incentives could be granted to support businesses adapting their workplaces or facilities to strengthened sanitary protocols.

Tax stimulus should be aligned with inclusive growth objectives and regressive tax stimulus should be avoided. As mentioned, this may be achieved by targeting tax relief (or other forms of income support) at lower income households. It may also involve providing additional relief to families with children. Tax stimulus aligned with inclusiveness objectives also implies avoiding providing tax relief that will predominantly benefit higher-income households, for instance through regressive personal income tax expenditures. This is particularly the case given that some high-income earners have benefited from the crisis and that this crisis has increased income polarisation (Stewart, McCarty and Bryson, 2020[28]; Stiglitz, 2020[29]; Bottan, Hoffmann and Vera-Cossio, 2020[30]). Governments should also favour tax support in the form of tax credits rather than tax allowances whose value increases with an individual's income level.

Tailoring stimulus to countries' specific circumstances

Stimulus policies should take into account country-specific needs. As mentioned in Chapter 1, countries have been unevenly affected by the crisis and the pace and scale of the recovery is also expected to vary widely across countries. Stimulus packages will need to be calibrated to the size of countries' output gaps. The timing of stimulus measures will also vary across countries, as some have already seen a pick-up in economic activity, while others are still imposing highly restrictive supply and demand constraints.

Stimulus should be aligned with countries' means. Countries entered the crisis with very different fiscal positions, including budget balances and government debt levels. In addition, their ability to rely on central bank support has varied. These financing constraints should be taken into consideration in designing stimulus policies. While limited stimulus may result in a slow economic recovery, disproportionate stimulus packages compared to countries' available fiscal space may undermine market confidence, which could result in lower investment and consumption, and weigh on the recovery. Evidence shows that fiscal multipliers tend to be smaller when fiscal positions are weaker (Huidrom et al., 2019[31]). It should be mentioned, however, that the near-term fiscal space has risen in many countries thanks to declining servicing costs.

Coordinating tax stimulus with other policies

Tax stimulus has to be designed in coordination with other crisis support measures, including wage subsidies, cash transfers, additional loans and debt guarantees. Tax stimulus – and fiscal policy more generally – also need to be carefully coordinated with monetary policy. Tax support will be the most effective if it is aligned with, and possibly reinforces the impact of, other support measures that countries have implemented.

Ideally, tax stimulus should be aligned with measures that will be taken over time to restore public finances and to address long-term challenges. Short term stimulus measures should be aligned with the direction that the tax system will need to take in the longer term. For instance, tax stimulus that would induce firms to invest in technology that is not environmentally friendly has to be avoided as it is not aligned with the optimal design of the tax system and the long-term objective of CO_2 neutrality.

Coordinating tax stimulus across countries

Fiscal policies have important output spill-over effects from one country to another. One lesson from the global financial crisis is that policy actions can have positive or negative externalities across countries. Economic support by some countries can create positive feedback loops through trade and investment links, providing a boost to the global economy (OECD, 2019[32]). Similarly, there could be negative feedback loops and negative externalities through integrated financial markets where countries in tight fiscal circumstances take limited expansionary fiscal action to help their economy to recover.

Therefore coordination of fiscal policies may valuable, particularly as openness increases. The benefits of internationally coordinated policy action can be seen from the experience of the global financial crisis, particularly in relation to monetary policy and financial market regulation. Fiscal policy would also benefit from a similarly coordinated approach.

3.2. In the medium run, tax and spending policies should be reassessed

The short-term priority is to continue navigating the pandemic and build a robust and inclusive recovery, but countries will need to start thinking about the medium and long-term challenges they face. Once the recovery is firmly in place, the post-crisis environment will provide an opportunity for countries to undertake a more fundamental reassessment of their tax and spending policies along with their overall fiscal framework. Such a reassessment should take into account both the challenges brought to the fore by the crisis as well as those related to ongoing structural trends. Such a reassessment should go beyond a focus on economic growth only, but integrate other key objectives of fiscal policy including inclusiveness, health, resilience and environmental sustainability.

Countries are facing a number of long-term structural challenges, including climate change, rising health risks, digitalisation, population ageing and increasing inequalities. Some of these challenges are interrelated, and some have been influenced by the COVID-19 crisis (e.g. accelerating digitalisation, inequalities). These trends can affect public finances in many ways: they can affect them directly (e.g. population ageing); they can influence the policy priorities of countries in the post-crisis environment; and they can have an effect on the different tax and spending policy instruments that are available (e.g. ageing populations and increases in automation or non-standard work may erode the personal income tax and social security contributions base over time).

Rethinking countries' public finance strategies will involve a combination of measures to support sustainable tax revenues and improve the quality of public spending, including through improved public finance governance. For some countries, increased domestic resource mobilisation will be needed to fund additional spending, whereas in countries with higher current levels of taxation and spending, there may be a need to contain spending growth, reprioritise spending and increase its efficiency. Tax revenues can be supported and enhanced with measures within the tax system (e.g. adjusting tax rates, broadening tax bases), but also with structural reforms (e.g. better education and training, reforms in the labour and product markets) that are not directly related to taxation but would support long-term economic growth and, in turn, growing tax bases.

The options to restore public finances will depend heavily on country-specific circumstances, including the country's starting point in terms of growth, development, inequalities and fiscal space; its current levels and structures of taxation and spending; as well as the nature of the specific long-term structural trends and challenges it faces. Those circumstances can vary widely across countries. For instance, countries at an earlier stage of economic development may have a lower tax-to-GDP ratio and have less developed social safety nets. Equally, countries may face different demographic challenges. For example, many OECD countries are facing considerable upward pressure on pension, health care and long-term care spending, whereas demography may have a more favourable effect on public finances in some emerging and developing economies.

Inclusive growth will also need to be at the heart of post-crisis tax policy. In addition to the benefits of growth for well-being and prosperity, robust growth rates support debt sustainability, by supporting tax revenues and eroding past debt. At the same time, policies will have to be inclusive and address inequalities. Recent studies have highlighted the negative impacts of the crisis on inequality (OECD, 2021[13]). Labour market outcomes have polarised, with those sectors affected by confinement measures having suffered sizeable income losses, while labour markets for some higher-income workers have hardly deteriorated at all (OECD, 2020[4]; Palomino, Rodriguez and Sebastian, 2020[5]). At the same time, asset prices have increased in many economies. In this context, the OECD will be undertaking work with a specific focus on personal capital taxation and the taxation of high income earners.

Countries will also need to address the challenges and seize the opportunities arising from digitalisation. Rising pressure on public finances as well as increased demands for fair burden sharing should provide new impetus for reaching an international agreement on how to address the tax challenges arising from the digitalisation of the economy. In the current context, international tax cooperation is even more important to ensure that tax disputes do not turn into trade wars, which would further harm recovery at a time when the global economy can least afford it. Work has continued to address the tax challenges arising from the digitalisation under the auspices of the OECD/G20 Inclusive Framework. In 2019, the Inclusive Framework agreed to a two-pillar Programme of Work that could form the basis for a multilateral consensus-based approach. Pillar One aims to expand the taxing rights of market jurisdictions where there is an active and sustained participation of a business in the economy of that jurisdiction. Pillar Two would introduce global anti-base erosion rules to ensure a minimum level of effective taxation. During the course of 2020, despite the COVID-19 pandemic, significant progress was made on the development of both Pillars. The Inclusive Framework approved Blueprint Reports on Pillar One and Pillar Two in October 2020 and released an Economic Impact Assessment of the proposals. At the same time, the Inclusive Framework also invited public comments on these Blueprint Reports in January 2021. The Inclusive Framework is building upon this input to further refine and simplify the Pillar One and Pillar Two proposals, with the objective of reaching a political agreement in mid-2021. In addition, broadening VAT bases by including all e-commerce, following the recommendations included in the OECD International VAT/GST Guidelines, is another priority to level the playing field between domestic and non-resident suppliers and has become even more important with the acceleration of digitalisation during the pandemic. Further, the increasing use of digital solutions can also play a key role in improving the functioning of tax administrations, as well as the design and implementation of tax policies.

Ensuring that the recovery is sustainable will be another major priority, which will involve, among other reforms, greater carbon pricing efforts. Today, taxes on polluting fuels are nowhere near the levels needed to encourage a shift towards clean energy. Around 70% of energy-related CO_2 emissions from advanced and emerging economies are entirely untaxed and some of the most polluting fuels remain among the least taxed (OECD, 2019[33]). This provides limited incentives for investors and citizens to favour clean over polluting energy sources. Adjusting taxes, along with state subsidies and investment, are therefore central elements of countries' strategies to curb carbon emissions. At the same time, policy packages should take account of the potential adverse impacts of carbon pricing on equity and affordability. The OECD will continue to build on its expertise to inform and support carbon pricing reform, adapted to countries' circumstances, in ways that strike a balance between creating incentives to reach carbon neutrality by the middle of the century, boosting inclusiveness and supporting sound public finances.

References

Baiardi, D., M. Magnani and M. Menegatti (2019), "The theory of precautionary saving: an overview of recent developments", *Review of Economics of the Household*, Vol. 18/2, pp. 513-542, http://dx.doi.org/10.1007/s11150-019-09460-3. [20]

Bartsch, E., A. Bénassy-Quéré and G. Corset (2020), *It's All In The Mix: How Monetary & Fiscal Policies Can Work Or Fail Together*, https://cepr.org/sites/default/files/geneva_reports/GenevaP334.pdf. [12]

BNP Paribas (2021), *Germany: Income Uncertainty Boosts Precautionary Savings*, https://economic-research.bnpparibas.com/Views/DisplayPublication.aspx?type=document&IdPdf=40638. [21]

Broda, C. and J. Parker (2014), "The economic stimulus payments of 2008 and the aggregate demand for consumption", *Journal of Monetary Economics*, Vol. 68/S, pp. S20-S36, http://dx.doi.org/10.1016/j.jmoneco.2014.09.002. [18]

Christiano, L., M. Eichenbaum and S. Rebelo (2011), "When Is the Government Spending Multiplier Large?", *Journal of Political Economy*, Vol. 119/1, pp. 78-121, http://dx.doi.org/10.1086/659312. [8]

Coenen, G. et al. (2012), "Effects of Fiscal Stimulus in Structural Models", *American Economic Journal: Macroeconomics*, Vol. 4/1, pp. 22-68, http://dx.doi.org/10.1257/mac.4.1.22. [10]

Edge, R. and J. Rudd (2011), "General-equilibrium effects of investment tax incentives", *Journal of Monetary Economics*, Vol. 58/6-8, pp. 564-577, http://dx.doi.org/10.1016/j.jmoneco.2011.10.007. [22]

Erceg, C. and J. Lindé (2014), "Is There A Fiscal Free Lunch In A Liquidity Trap?", *Journal of the European Economic Association*, Vol. 12/1, pp. 73-107, http://dx.doi.org/10.1111/jeea.12059. [11]

European Commission (2020), *Coronavirus response: Commission welcomes agreement on crucial VAT relief for vaccines and testing kits*, https://ec.europa.eu/commission/presscorner/detail/en/ip_20_2299. [2]

Guerini, M. et al. (2020), "Firm liquidity and solvency under the Covid-19 lockdown in France", *OFCE Policy Brief*, Vol. 76, https://www.ofce.sciences-po.fr/pdf/pbrief/2020/OFCEpbrief76.pdf. [6]

Huidrom, R. et al. (2019), *Why Do Fiscal Multipliers Depend on Fiscal Positions?*, World Bank, Washington, DC, http://dx.doi.org/10.1596/1813-9450-8784. [31]

IMF (2020), *Whatever It Takes: Europe's Response to COVID-19*, IMF Publishing, Washington, DC, https://doi.org/10.5089/9781513558233.086. [24]

Joe, W. (ed.) (2020), "The unequal impact of the coronavirus pandemic: Evidence from seventeen developing countries", *PLOS ONE*, Vol. 15/10, p. e0239797, http://dx.doi.org/10.1371/journal.pone.0239797. [30]

Maffini, G., J. Xing and M. Devereux (2019), "The Impact of Investment Incentives: Evidence from UK Corporation Tax Returns", *American Economic Journal: Economic Policy*, Vol. 11/3, pp. 361-389, http://dx.doi.org/10.1257/pol.20170254. [25]

Mody, A., F. Ohnsorge and D. Sandri (2012), "Precautionary Savings in the Great Recession", *IMF Economic Review*, Vol. 60/1, pp. 114-138, http://www.jstor.org/stable/41427964. [19]

OECD (2021), *OECD Economic Outlook, Interim Report March 2021*, OECD Publishing, Paris, https://dx.doi.org/10.1787/34bfd999-en. [13]

OECD (2020), *COVID-19: Protecting people and societies*, OECD Publishing, Paris, https://doi.org/10.1787/5b0fd8cd-en. [3]

OECD (2020), *Green budgeting and tax policy tools to support a green recovery*, OECD Publishing, Paris, https://doi.org/10.1787/5b0fd8cd-en. [26]

OECD (2020), *Insolvency and debt overhang following the COVID-19 outbreak: Assessment of risks and policy responses*, OECD Publishing, Paris, https://doi.org/10.1787/7806f078-en. [7]

OECD (2020), *OECD Employment Outlook 2020: Worker Security and the COVID-19 Crisis*, OECD Publishing, Paris, https://dx.doi.org/10.1787/1686c758-en. [4]

OECD (2019), "Focus Note 4: Global policy co-operation is needed in the event of a deeper downturn", OECD Publishing, Paris, https://dx.doi.org/10.1787/c8a9590d-en. [32]

OECD (2019), *Taxing Energy Use 2019: Using Taxes for Climate Action*, OECD Publishing, Paris, https://dx.doi.org/10.1787/058ca239-en. [33]

Palomino, J., J. Rodriguez and R. Sebastian (2020), *Wage inequality and poverty effects of lockdown and social distancing in Europe*, https://www.inet.ox.ac.uk/files/Lockdown_inequality_Palomino_Rodriguez_Sebastian_WP.pdf . [5]

Parker, J. et al. (2013), "Consumer spending and the economic stimulus payments of 2008", *American Economic Review*, Vol. 103/6, pp. 2530-2553, http://dx.doi.org/10.1257/aer.103.6.2530. [17]

Ramey, V. (2019), "Ten Years After the Financial Crisis: What Have We Learned from the Renaissance in Fiscal Research?", *Journal of Economic Perspectives*, Vol. 33/2, pp. 89-114, http://dx.doi.org/10.1257/jep.33.2.89. [1]

Sahm, C., M. Shapiro and J. Slemrod (2010), *Check in the Mail or More in the Paycheck: Does the Effectiveness of Fiscal Stimulus Depend on How It Is Delivered?*, National Bureau of Economic Research, Cambridge, MA, http://dx.doi.org/10.3386/w16246. [16]

Schnabel, I. (2021), *Unconventional fiscal and monetary policy at the zero lower bound*, https://www.ecb.europa.eu/press/key/date/2021/html/ecb.sp210226~ff6ad267d4.en.html. [15]

Stewart, A., N. McCarty and J. Bryson (2020), "Polarization under rising inequality and economic decline", *Science Advances*, Vol. 6/50, p. eabd4201, http://dx.doi.org/10.1126/sciadv.abd4201. [28]

Stiglitz, J. (2020), *IMF Finance & Development: Conquering the Great Divide - The pandemic has laid bare deep divisions, but it's not too late*, https://www.imf.org/external/pubs/ft/fandd/2020/09/pdf/COVID19-and-global-inequality-joseph-stiglitz.pdf. [29]

US Treasury (2010), *The Case For Temporary 100 Percent Expensing: Encouraging Business To Expand Now By Lowering The Cost of Investment*, https://home.treasury.gov/system/files/131/Report-Temporary-100percent-Expensing-2010.pdf. [14]

Van Dender, K. and J. Teusch (2020), "Making environmental tax reform work", *La Revue des Juristes de Sciences Po*, Vol. 18, pp. 106-111, http://revuedesjuristes-desciencespo.com. [27]

Woodford, M. (2011), "Simple Analytics of the Government Expenditure Multiplier", *American Economic Journal: Macroeconomics*, Vol. 3/1, pp. 1-35, http://dx.doi.org/10.1257/mac.3.1.1. [9]

Zwick, E. and J. Mahon (2017), "Tax Policy and Heterogeneous Investment Behavior", *American Economic Review*, Vol. 107/1, pp. 217-248, http://dx.doi.org/10.1257/aer.20140855. [23]

9 789264 625655